hello gorgeous

BE INSPIRED

NIKKI TAYLOR

Copyright © 2017

All rights reserved. This book or any portion thereof may not be reproduced or used in any manner whatsoever without the express written permission of the author except for the use of brief quotations in a book review.
Cover design: Troy Viray

Printed in Australia
First Printing, 2017
ISBN: 978-0-6481476-3-3
White Light Publishing House
Hillside, VIC, Australia 3037
whitelightpublishing.com.au

We are daughters, friends, wives, mothers, sisters, aunts, nieces, grandmothers, granddaughters, cousins, girlfriends, daughters-in-law, friends and ladyboss.

I personally Dedicate my book to:

Trixie my adorable quirky grandmother who styled herself every day and Thelma my nana who had the best gardens and dress up clothes ever!

Rossie my mum – she was one truly special lady, as all of these women were, she was a mum that was a born entrepreneur with so much creative flair.

The four special men in my life, my two sons Adam and Sam, my stepson Jono and my husband Richard who has helped me with this book from inception to reality.

Soul sisters friends to me, who are like my true sisters that I never had, you know who you all are and thank you. A special mention to Ana, like a real sisterhood friend that I didn't have, you may always be in another country, the distance never stops our conversations.

Jacqui, mother of my granddaughter and an amazing mother to her girls Bella, with amazing creativity and Milly with so much attitude and personality.

Olivia my step daughter, she has the love of learning, a quirky attitude and a HUGE heart. Currently she is bringing more inspiring women into the world as a midwife.

Claire, Sophie and Rose my beautiful nieces – just like their aunty.

Zoe and Briar my great nieces with loads of attitude and personality – I am so proud of them.

My two cousins that I can call friends Lynette and Christine, you are always there for me and for each other. Amelia, Christine's daughter, with model features and a gorgeous smile and Jeanette and Deborah, Lynette's daughters always interested in others and narratives of hope & transformation.

To all my aunties out there I love you all.

To my sister in law married to my brother Terry, along with her sister and sister in laws all in New Zealand, a special mention to you lovely ladies.

Lastly a very special mention to my step sister in law Ange thank you for being you and always being there.

CONTENTS

Midlife Turning Points — 12
Anne Noonan – Australia

Estella's Brilliant Bus — 14
Estella Pyfrom – USA

Get Inspired to Eat and Live Well — 16
Marni Wasserman – Canada

Be True To Yourself — 20
Ana Pristopan – Romania

A Mother's Journey in Resilience & Gold — 24
Pam Cleverley – New Zealand

Living with IT — 28
Paula Brand – Australia

A New Adventure — 30
Justine Asher – South Africa

Almost Six Years of Passion — 32
Saija Mahon – UK

Leading Women — 34
Christina Guidotti – Australia

Disarm Your Limits   38
Jessica Cox – USA

Graceful Life Transitions   42
Dr. Micaela Becattini – Australia

Life Can Change in an Instant   46
Jacqui Kalka – New Zealand

Understanding Your Strengths is The Key to Success   48
Sara Redman – Australia

How to be a SoloPreneur in 7 Steps   52
Jeany Park – USA

Empowering Women to Become the Masters of Their Own Destiny Post Domestic Violence   54
Kate Worsfold – Australia

Anything is Possible   56
Carmen Harrison and Cassandra Rathgeber – Canada

Discovering Your Inner Compass   58
Zoë Routh – Australia

Stepping Into the Unknown Can Be Worthwhile   62
Sue Stockdale – UK

Finding Freedom Within   66
Ruby Usman – Australia

I am known in the business world as "Allie" — 70
Maritess Pasag – Philippines

Keep Your Eye on the Ball — 74
Dr. Sherylle Calder – South Africa

I made Google love me — 76
Kate Toon – Australia

An Advocate and Champion for Other Women — 78
Ndidi Nwuneli – Nigeria

Change Maker — 82
Dina Cooper – Australia

Viva Health and Wealth — 84
Mandie Spooner – Australia

Moms and More — 86
Drs. Nikolien Martina-Doorenbos – Netherlands

Thinking Happy — 90
Jenny Strong – Australia

Life is an Adventure — 92
Karen Darke – UK

Discover Your Why — 94
Christine Rudolph – Australia

Be The Best You Can Be — 98
Cassandra Austin – Australia

Game Changer — 102
Kate Maree O'Brien – New Zealand

More Time, More Freedom and More Money — 104
Sharon Jurd – Australia

Mom On A Mission — 106
Lisa Druxman – USA

Honour Your Journey, Create Your Life — 108
Narelle Shiell – Australia

Stay True To Yourself — 112
Tracey Mathers – Australia

Juggling a Virtual Career while Being a Full Time Wife and Mom — 116
Grace Alviar Viray – Philippines

Serve, Surrender, Impact — 118
Hershey Hilado – Australia

On Fire for Healthy Eating: From Passion to Mission — 120
Dina Del Rosario Josue – Philippines

The Real Deal — 124
Gaby McEwan – Australia

What Defines Someone Who Is Inspirational? — 128
Phillippa Jacobs – New Zealand

**Why 1000 Self Help Books Won't Set
Women Fully Free. Discover the MAZ Factor**   **132**

Maz Schirmer – Australia

Life can Change in the Blink of an Eye!   **136**

Julie Sawchuk – Canada

A Strong Intuition and Ability to Heal   **138**

Liz La Force – Ibiza

**Living Life Positively Courageous,
with Femininity & Style!**   **140**

Deborah Johnston – Australia

Push Past Your Limits   **144**

Pauleanna Reid – Canada

Why Your Story Matters   **146**

Suzie Lightfoot – Australia

Freedom Lifestyle – Don't Hold Me Back   **151**

Nikki Taylor – Australia

I Never Lost Sight Of What I Wanted To Do   **154**

Tina Banitska – Australia

Magnetic Branding   **158**

Zahrina Robertson – Australia

**Nipples to Nowhere – One Woman's Journey
of Health and Recovery**   **162**

Kathy Ashton – Australia

Anne Noonan Bio

Anne Noonan, Integrative Wellness Yogini inspires, motivates and coaches the 50+ woman to believe that her second half of life can be as flexible, healthy, agile, sexy, successful and strong as her first half of life. Anne has worked with hundreds of clients over 20+ years helping them bring out their Personal Styling, Fashion, Makeup tuition and Personal Branding skills.

But more recently as a certified Nutrition, Food, Yoga and Stretch coach, Anne works with the 40 and 50+ and beyond to Roll back their Internal Odometer. Anne's own health journey with menopause and all that it brings, has inspired her to prove that rather than an uncomfortable experience it can actually be the doorway to a magnificently vibrant time of life.

Midlife Turning Points

Anne Noonan – Australia

Our second half of life can be so much better than the first. I truly believe that we can turn our health completely around if we grab hold of it in time. And when we do, our whole life can change. Relationships, business, personal success and our purpose can turn up in amazing ways.

At the age of about 46 I found myself facing a hysterectomy. I was excited about it. I just wanted this hell of a cycle that began at the age of 11 to be over. When my cycle began in primary school it determined where I went, what invitations I accepted, whether I went swimming when everyone else was going or whether I spent a lot of time at home.

It remained that way throughout my life. I accepted it as normal – doesn't everyone have ridiculously heavy painful periods?? A few years and 2 kids later, when a hysterectomy was suggested, I was over it. I was over the anaemia, the fatigue, the deficiencies, the weight gain, the weird illnesses and the depression that accompanied it – I was ready.

This was it! It was going to be done and I was going to have my life back.

It wasn't to be. I woke up out of the anaesthetic in a hot flush and my menopausal symptoms seemed to be on full volume. Hot flushes that didn't seem to end. Dry skin, sore joints, increasing middle, overloaded liver, foggy thinking, lack of interest in everything and a feeling of simply sinking deeper into a pit.

I wanted out of it. My gyno suggested I go see my local for an HRT script, I had my doctor suggest antidepressants and in my foggy hot sweaty brain I was ready to give up. A couple of naturopaths gave me different treatments all of which treated a little section of a whole – like spraying a raging fire with a squirter bottle.

So it was time to step up and take my life into my own hands.

I had my certificate in human nutrition, I knew my stuff, I knew how to eat healthily and I thought I was. It just wasn't enough. The real detective work began in earnest! I studied up every book, seminar, CD and workshop I could get hold of that concentrated on the midlife woman and the issues she deals with. From anxiety to zinc deficiency I had to take my health by the reigns and turn it around.

So I did. It took a few years, some experimentation and some failings. My body became my petri dish. When I learned about the liver, the importance of macro and micro nutrition, the power of breath and movement, my health did an about face. Weight dropped off, my fogginess disappeared, my skin cleared up, the fatigue lifted and my achiness was replaced with a sheer joy for life.

I now run programs for women who've gone through something similar. You can turn back the clock – you can regain your vitality. I want to live life to the fullest until it's time to go. Doesn't everyone? With a nutrition and mindful movement plan it's doable. When I discovered mindful movement and breath techniques it was like my cells started singing 'hallelujah, she's found what she needs'. So I became a yoga and meditation instructor and combine it with my health coaching and have a driving passion now for the midlife woman who wants her mojo back.

Estella Pyfrom Bio

Estella's Brilliant Bus, formerly known as Project Aspiration, is a customized mobile learning center, designed to travel to communities and deliver services to children and families throughout the state of Florida, nation and world.

In order to make the vision become a reality, Estella Pyfrom invested a large sum of her pension money into the project. She is confident that the project is helping to improve the quality of life for children and families and is making a difference…one child at a time and/or one family at a time.

Estella's Brilliant Bus

Estella Pyfrom – USA

My name is Estella Pyfrom. I am the CEO and Founder of Estella's Brilliant Bus (not for profit organization). I am the second oldest of six daughters and one son. My father, Roy L. Mims, was a migrant worker, a crew leader and a camp manager for many years. As a kid my family and I traveled for nineteen (19) years, transporting migrant workers from Florida to New York, by driving trucks and buses to the camps. As a village kid, I was inspired to give back to my village (my community).

As an adult, I worked very hard in my community and was a dedicated wife and mother to my children and to many other children in my neighborhood circle.

After raising four children and teaching them how to stay out of trouble, my accomplishment that I am proudest of is the Creation and founding of Estella's Brilliant Bus. … AWESOME because we are mobile and virtual and can learn anywhere in the world. We're a learning center without walls… no boundaries. The learning center travels to communities where service is needed. We will make a difference…one child at a time and/or one family at a time.

I believe that by forming alliances with agencies in communities who have similar missions and who have been awarded grants, have grant funds to provide services can form partnerships to serve hard to reach individuals and all will benefit from the union. The learning center travels to communities where service is needed. Estella will continue to seek financial assistance and continue to collaborative community stakeholders provide resources to help improve the quality of life for children and families who are in need of our services. We will make a difference…one child at a time and/or one family at a time.

I am proud to say we have served more than 100,000 underserved children over the past four years and have not charged them any money.

During the first year after we started this Brilliant Bus Movement Business, my husband became a victim of a triage visit at a local hospital which landed him in ICU for two months that required me to be with him (in ICU) for 24 hours in order to help keep him alive. In spite of all of our assistance at the hospital, he survived 4 cases of CODE Blue and 26 pints of blood transfusion. Luckily he survived resuscitation, four times. Thank God he is still here… well and alive. In August of 2013 both my husband and I were victims of an automobile accident, when a texting driver t-bowed us as we were driving out of our development. Yes, they ran the red light. As result of that accident, my husband was 98% paralysed and had to have an emergency spinal surgery. As for me, I got away with only one broken hip, and injured knee and ankle and a battered face to the point that my children could not recognise me. But to God be the Glory, WE ARE BOTH ALIVE TODAY.

When I look back over her past and begin to think of what attributes to my success in life, all I could think of is the "no failure" options that was instilled in me as a child by my father. . My dad made all of us believe that if you could dream, … dream Big, and work hard to make your dreams become realities… Failure was not an option.

During the past four years we have been very celebrated for our hard work.

Marni Wasserman Bio

Simply said, Marni Wasserman's life is rooted in healthy living. She is a Culinary Nutritionist & Co-Host of The Ultimate Health Podcast. She is also the Author of the books *"Fermenting for Dummies"* and *"Plant-Based Diet For Dummies"*.

Marni has also made several media appearances on Breakfast Television, Global News, CBC, CHCH and Newstalk 1010 and has articles in the National Post, Toronto Star, Huffington Post and Chatelaine Magazine. Marni uses passion and experience to educate individuals on how to adopt a balanced real food diet and a wholesome lifestyle through simple strategies.

Get Inspired to Eat and Live Well

Marni Wasserman – Canada

To put it as simply as possible, I love to eat and live well. More than anything I love to share my passion and knowledge to live the healthiest life possible.

As cliché as that sounds, it's true. This drive to make "the world" a healthier place started with a foundation in the area of kinesiology and health sciences. I then became a personal trainer and after talking to people about how to eat for optimal health, I realized this wasn't enough. People needed to learn and see what was involved in taking control of their health.

The only logical next step for me at this time was to attend school for holistic nutrition and then culinary school. These two programs fueled my desire to start teaching my own cooking classes. There was a demand for people to learn how to make and prepare their own foods at home and I saw that need and I wanted to be that person.

When I first started, I didn't have a plan or the know-how to run a business I just knew I wanted to get as many people "healthy" as possible. So in the kitchen of my parent's home, my little cooking class business began. I started doing weekly health focused cooking classes; I led retreats, hosted events and started to circulate around my city and others to facilitate talks, workshops and cooking demonstrations. I was in my element. I not only got to share my passion for health and nutrition but I got to show people how to do it.

I was onto something, my classes were full and there was a request for more, I had to go bigger. I outgrew my parent's home and I decided to open up my own brick and mortar Food Studio. At the same time, I had two book deals; Plant-Based Diet and Fermenting for Dummies with very short deadlines. Not to mention while this was all happening I was going through a divorce.

This massive shift in my personal life motivated me to create the best food studio that I could have possibly imagined. So I did it. I built a high end beautiful kitchen from scratch which became a hub to connect people through food. I succeeded. It was my dream come true. However, just like any dream, it must come to an end as a new one begins to take its place.

I am actually just in the middle of letting my food studio go. I have outgrown it and ready to escalate my abilities to more than just teach cooking classes. I am ready to reach people on a global level. With the experience that I have in building communities and transforming people's health through food, I am ready to apply this knowledge in new and exciting ways. I have come to learn that health is more than just what goes into your mouth, it's your lifestyle, the people you associate with and the choices you make day to day.

Shortly after opening up the studio, I met my now partner Jesse Chappus. In contrast to my previous relationship, this guy was like the male version of me. Sharing all my same passions, morals and values about life and health. It was inevitable we would create something together – thus the birth of The Ultimate Health Podcast which we now co-host together.

What first started out as a "side" project has now grown into a full time business. Jesse, once a chiropractor has now left his practice for the upward swing of the podcast.

The podcast is more than a weekly health show; it is a community and collection of people looking to inspire and be inspired. With the show reaching over a million people we have the chance to get a message out about health and wellness in a practical, fun and helpful way. With guests such as Dr Mark Hyman, Gretchen Rubin, Arianna Huffington and Deepak Chopra we cover a wide range of topics allowing the listener to come to their own conclusions without pushing any agenda.

I am excited to see what comes of this new transition in my life. One thing I have learned is that it is so important to stay open minded, as you never know what will come at you. Life is a set of experiences that help us to grow, evolve and expand. Just stay clear on your initial goals and you will get to where you want to go, just not always in a linear way.

"Breathe. Let go. And remind yourself that this very moment is the only one you know you have for sure."
Oprah Winfrey

Ana Pristopan Bio

Ana is well known for her good sense of humour, friendly nature and she makes a positive impression on everyone she meets. Her people skills are exceptional and are a major contributor to her success in real estate. She is a fully licensed real estate agent, studying towards a Diploma in Business and Management.

With more than 20 years' experience in management and sales, Ana is passionate and truly committed to maximising the value of her clients' real estate assets through superior customer service. As an ex sales manager and a licensee agent, she utilises and passes on her skills, knowledge and success to the people she works with.

Ana began her selling career in Europe 30 years ago. There she gained a Bachelor of Commerce and ran her own business for more than 11 years. Because Ana has been self-employed, she is well organised, self-motivated and sets high standards of professional service.

Always striving for perfection, Ana doesn't tolerate mistakes in a relationship and is known for her high standards of professional service, negotiating skills, integrity and enthusiasm. Perseverance and focus are crucial for Ana – she never gives up and is with you every step of the way.

Be True To Yourself

Ana Pristopan – Romania

When I have decided to leave my home, I have decided to do it for my children. I wanted a better life for them and myself. I have never thought of leaving my home country for 39 years. After a difficult marriage break I made a decision to leave everything behind, even though I was running a very successful business for more than 11 years. I have built that business from scratch selling first from a garage then turn it into a wholesale deposit. There is nothing that is more frightening and more challenging than to leave all you know for the fearful of the unknown.

On the night of 5th of February 2000 everything changed … I left Romania and my 2 children behind in my parent's care to go and live in New Zealand. A country I have chosen just pointing my finger on the map saying I am going there in the end the world. I had only $400 in my pocket after a bad divorce in which everything was taken from me and did not know anybody in NZ. It would be too risky to take my children with me and expose them to the unknown. It was the hardest decision that I had to make. But I knew and trusted that everything will be ok and I will see them soon. And I am so happy I did…

I cannot not even describe the fear and tears that has been inside my heart on the plane ride. I was holding my prayer book all the time and prayed, cried and prayed…for 33 hours… God gave me the power to believe that I did the right choice and one day I will see my children again. I believed that this was for the greater good that my children knew how much I adore them and that one-day this day would come, the day that we could all be together again.

I struggled to find a job but found a lovely Hungarian family who took me under their wings and looked after me until I found a job. I was and still am very blessed and lucky. Beside the nanny jobs, I was doing cleaning jobs and living in a stranger's home looking after 3 children.

The small offerings that a strange family have given me, slowly felt like home, it had to, because for my two beautiful children that I left behind, I must power through with hope that one day they will be beside me.

I've dreamed every night that this will lead to bigger and better things. Perseverance is what pays, it pays to dream, even if reality never paid as much.

It became harder and harder to accept that a paycheck from someone else for doing their dirty housework was enough, so I've set my foot to do something that will one day allow me to become the person I am today.

I got my dream job that allowed me to show the world my personality, to speak to those that were prepared to pay the big bucks for my hope. I have dreamed to get into management and one day to run successfully my own business. And I did…

Today, this is the journey of the woman who is running very successfully her own franchise, this is the journey of a single mum ready to take on the world to prove she can make those dreams (from the granny flat of some rich person's home) come true.

Along the journey there were obstacles, and boy were they tough. Not only that I could not see my children growing older, but they also needed my support. This came to me effortlessly because they were the sunshine of my life and gave me strengths not to give up.

My sweet parents taught me well, they have held my back and pushed me forward enough times to realize what my heart desired, and I went for it.

A few people have tried to hold me back, but they have all failed. "Because nothing has power over you unless you let it, absolutely nothing". I was a new immigrant with a funny accent and with a difficult surname (one of my bosses even asked me to change my name if I want to work there and be successful). I've decided I don't need to…and left. An immigrant who knew only one person in NZ and wanted to work in real estate, so she had to work very hard cause she was grateful that she could be there to start a new life with her children. That's what kept me going.

It is a treasure to be true to yourself in today's world, because putting on a brave face is not so easy. Even as life went on and even with those that held me back I've made a beautiful decision.

I am very grateful to all the people from NZ and to a country, which allowed me to change to have a fresh new life and to see my children after 2 years. I am so blessed. Thank you New Zealand!

When you get a letter like this from your children, you know that you did a good job and I am so proud and speechless:

> …"To this day your sacrifices, your struggles and your pain have made you the beautiful person you were destined to be. They have allowed us to call you MUM. Now our dear MUM, that is a title. It may not come with gold medals and it may not pay the bills, but it is eternal. If at any time your journey comes to a hold and you must once again sacrifice, remember all that has

lead you to get to this day and remember that we are here. The promise of tomorrow will never be, but the promise of our love and compassion will always hold you up, that we promise you. We have always wondered what we did to deserve you, but I guess that will forever be a mystery, an unsolved puzzle that is a sight for sore eyes. The definition of love and trust came through your touch from the moment we were born, so we thank you for all that you have gone through and all that you will go through. For giving us life and giving us love we cannot repay you, but we will promise to forever make you proud for making the decision to be our inspiring mother. Your grace and prosperity will forever shine in our hearts!

WE LOVE YOU MUM"

(Vanessa and Sebastian Pristopan)

Pam Cleverley Bio

Pam has gone through many struggles over the last 10 years. far more than other mums, this story is a way of her connecting with the world about how you can get there if you keep on pushing.

You can find out more about Charlotte, her daughter at www.charlottecleverleybisman.com.

A Mother's Journey in Resilience & Gold
Pam Cleverley – New Zealand

Not in your wildest dreams could you imagine this journey. You wake up one day and it leads you to 5 months away from home. I am a single Mum of 3, Ruby, Riwa and Charlotte.

I worried about having a third child, but Charlotte was a delightful baby. Secure in her routine, happy, healthy and bubbly, bystanders would notice her and see her spirit. She was born in November of 2003, and entering into her 6th month on June 17th 2004, she woke at 3am, with vomiting and high temperature, I rushed to get her the appropriate meds, and she started a high pitch whimpering (a symptom not then mentioned, as a symptom).

We fell asleep together till morning, but little did I know she was in deep toxic shock. Waking, I let her sleep on, my gut feeling was worried, but I put it down to me being over protective, and with a sitter in place to oversee Charlotte I rushed Ruby and Riwa to school, and went to work for two hours.

Arriving home I was shocked to hear Charlotte was still sleeping and on closer investigation, I was shocked to see her in the same position I left her in, motionless, gazing, eyes half open, and two defined blood spots on her neck. Panic rose up my body, as I recognised the symptoms as Meningitis.

The story continues as written on her Dad's website.

Life changed that day, the feeling of helplessness and hopelessness was hard to endure. The emotion like having a jumbo jet fly over you while you lie paralyzed on the tarmac face up. We watched helplessly over Charlotte as she went to war with the most deadliest disease known to man. Hospital was our world for the next 3 months. Day/Night – we never knew, it just blended into continual highly stressful seconds, minutes, hours, days and months.

Our journey climaxed to a social media frenzy after a front page Herald paper headlined the Vaccine for the Meningitis B (which Charlotte was suffering) was about to be thrown out due to the nearing use-by date, along with $250 Million of taxpayers money. We contacted the Herald, Really – You have a Vaccine?

Get it out there that this is what it's doing to our baby. Charlotte's photo in the front page of the next morning's Herald paper, article written by Charlotte's father Perry. She was pictured happy on a swing. Holding on with hands. Balanced by legs, all now taken by this evil disease. New Zealanders we're mortified and demanded the vaccine. Which was soon released into all schools. Nurses left our ward to take part. Doctors thanked us.

Charlotte survived, she had nationwide interest in her well being and we were followed around by media. But we had our child, devastated by disease, a quad amputee, only her elbow to work with. We spent two months at a children's home to heal from skin grafts and debridement, and to adapt to Charlotte as a quadruple amputee.

One doctor, one day mentioned the journey will be a rocky road. Little did I know the journey, little did I know the road was, in fact, many mountains to climb. How much resilience does one need? For a baby to fight a deadly bacteria. For doctors and nurses to be in the operating theatre and save children's lives. For parents to endure the grief and guilt of their child's illness. To endure whatever trauma life gives you.

Now our 'Normal':

Battling the accessibility of businesses, inaccessible disabled car parks that have had no thought around their placement, disabled toilets that are locked or used as a storage lobby, public transport that is not accessible, governed limb centers on tight budgets and over loaded with patients exasperated by diabetic casualties, Carer Aids that are underpaid, unfit, and uneducated on a high-needs spectrum on the individuality of ORRS students, a Health and Safety law which confines parents of disabled children and entitles the removal of their mobility and free movement and speech. – To name some of the hurdles. The strength and endurance it takes. On top of the 24/7 care of a high-needs child.

My job title of now without the university degree : Activist for Human Rights, physio, mobility designer, and gadget designs, prosthetist, skin and scar management, employer, wages clerk, fundraiser, public speaker (TV and articles), assisting with infrastructure for access, researcher, environmentalist, nutritionist, mentor, carer, organiser of equipment repairs, appointments and meetings.

Without these ongoing challenges, I would not be the strong confident person I am today. Charlottes resilience and spirit, has enabled me to endure all challenges in our journey. When you mine for gold, there's a lot of hard work to find it. Similar to the strength and endurance you need to raise a quad amputee.

When the day flows, when Charlotte first swims, when she takes her first prosthetic leg steps, when she runs in blades, disabled surfing, skydiving, her incredible art, her happiness. That is my gold.

"Life shrinks or expands in proportion to one's courage."
Anais Nin

Paula Brand Bio

A Computer Chick, a Soldier, a Networking Lunch and Business Expo owner, Facebook Business Trainer and a dynamic people connector.

She is a single mother of a beautiful fijian, cook islander, aussie child and is a passionate foodie.

One of the things you may not know about Paula is that she was a not so good muslim wife.

Paula blends 24 years of industry development, sales, marketing and business skills to help grow small businesses in the North Gold Coast region to make them Shine-Connect- GROW.

She owns the North GC Business Expo and the South GC Business Expo as part of the Northern Gold Coast Business Networking Lunch Series which has no member fees and is open to all business owners.

Living with IT

Paula Brand – Australia

Some years are transformative ones where we burst out of our shells and gallop at such a rate that speeding light goes at a snail's pace.

2014 was such a year for me with the first month spent in the Domestic Violence court winning a DVO against my business partner who was also my life partner which left me in a wilderness of low self-esteem and fear of failure.

I struggled on with my six month old business start-up in an industry that I was unfamiliar with but loved from the moment I registered it.

Living with IT was created because I knew each home and business had a number of computers that would need computer repairs and servicing.

For twelve months I stood in survival mode and put one foot in front of the other to make enough money to pay bills and feed my six year old daughter and I.

I had to throw myself into the business world during school hours and so the North GC Business Lunch Series was created of which the lunch events are now sold out every month. It wasn't ego driving me, it was pure fear and desperation.

As I got into the rhythm of learning the business ropes, I had the good fortune to surround myself with business leaders and successful business supporters. I met the then Prime Minister Tony Abbott and a number of Federal Ministers and local and state members of Parliament as well as Gina Rinehart, the richest woman in Australia. These leaders gave me courage and inspiration to keep growing.

As a result, I founded and ran the North GC Business Expo in August 2014 which was a huge success for businesses in the fastest growing region of Australia. My ethos has always been "if you help enough people, then success will come".

As my confidence grew I sought out media to raise my profile, which I encourage all small business owners to do. My personal healing was moved along by being brave and standing on a platform in public and on social media to tell Gold Coast women, Domestic Violence has no place in our community.

A year on and I feel like a new person, I have scheduled in ME time and I am just about to launch the South GC Business Lunch Series as well as the South GC Business Expo. My Facebook Success Workshops will extend to run in Brisbane and Living with IT, my core business, has doubled its revenue.

From desperation comes inspiration and I am grateful for all the support I have received along my journey this year.

> **Justine Asher Bio**
>
> Justine Asher is Wife, Mother, Artist, Dreamer, and Para-Cyclist double world champion. She and her husband own a real estate company specialising in residential sales and rentals. She began para-cycling 2 years ago. Prior to cycling, she swam 2km a day at the Virgin Active in order to maintain her health and fitness.
>
> *"Never, in my 25 years of being a quadriplegic, have I experienced such challenge, freedom and reward as I have in para-cycling."*
>
> Justine hopes to inspire other women to take up para-cycling by creating awareness and bringing some exposure to the sport.

A New Adventure

Justine Asher – South Africa

At the age of 18, freshly out of high school my modelling career was blossoming and the dream of travelling to exotic locations across the world was at my fingertips. Now that my school days were behind me I was seduced by a sense of wanderlust and had the world at my feet.

I travelled from my hometown in Cape Town to Johannesburg, to join a top agency and shortly before landing a modelling contract in Milan I suffered a chronic spinal cord injury as a result of a car accident. I recall lying in hospital when I received the news and felt a deep sense of disappointment. I don't think the reality of my situation had quite set in.

Everything I had taken for granted became impossible, even the easiest of tasks such as scratching my head or feeding myself. I was told by the doctors that I would never walk again. Those words never quite resonated with me. During my months in hospital rehab I regained the use of my arms, and some use of my hands, but never regained my ability to walk again, remaining paralysed from my chest down with limited use of my hands.

I never gave up dreaming, hoping and desiring, but rather shifted my focus on all I could do and the impossible become my challenge.

Looking back, I marvel at what my life has become, I am now a mother of two teenage daughters and happily married for 18 years. My husband and I run a successful real estate company. I have had the wonderful experience of diving and excavating wrecks and I have swum alongside sharks in the Waterfront Aquarium.

When I turned 41, I decided to embark on a new adventure after a friend introduced me to para-cycling, just for the challenge and excitement of trying something new.

I use to love running and enjoyed the fresh air and being active out in nature and cycling came pretty much close to it. I loved the freedom and the feeling of the wind on my skin and being out on my bike with no limitations. Starting with only completing 4 km's, a ride to the beach and back, my first little hill felt like Mount Everest. Determined to push more and challenging myself each day to push further and take on bigger climbs and more challenging rides, eventually after persevering and lots of hard training, I was cycling 50 kms and climbing over 700m.

After joining Maties para-sports club, I entered Nationals and was fortunate to make the SA Para-cycling team and have now been cycling competitively on the international circuit for 4 years.

In 2014 after winning numerous sports awards including the prestigious SA Sportswoman of the Year with a Disability which was a great honour and privilege, I won the world champion title in both the road race and time trial in 2015. In 2016 I was selected to represent my country at the Paralympics in Rio.

My life has been and continues to be an amazing adventure, from travelling the globe to looking to some more exciting adventures. I feel immense gratitude and a wonderful sense of achievement and not for a moment do I live in regret, but rather live each day as if it were my last.

I am fortunate to be blessed with a wonderful family and friends and every day is a new day worth celebrating. My proudest moments are when I see my children following their passions with purpose and never losing their sense of self-esteem and I hope that I have been successful at leading by example.

Saija Mahon Bio

Saija Mahon is the founder of Mahon Digital Marketing Ltd, an international, award-winning digital media agency that helps growing global businesses to achieve their sales targets by utilising advanced technologies and strategical tactics in the ever expanding online environment.

After working for some of the biggest global media houses in the world, Saija decided to launch her own business 6 years ago, starting her journey as an entrepreneur from London, UK. Mahon Digital Marketing specialises specifically in biddable media, website optimisation, search engine optimisation, content marketing, social media optimisation and PR activities. Mahon Digital operates their main offices from London UK and also Turku Finland, with multiple resources across US, Europe and Asia. And this is only the beginning.

Almost Six Years of Passion

Saija Mahon – UK

As during the 'honeymoon' period of any relationship, I've noticed I talk about my business rather the same way – with passion, with exact knowledge of how long this great relationship has been going on, and with endless energy and effort to ensure it all keeps going strong for many years to come.

Owning and running a business is pretty much a lifestyle, you need to love it, and you need to immerse yourself fully in it.

There's no denying being a business owner is challenging, and like any relationship – it has its ups and downs. You keep on learning each day as you go along, and that's truly the real excitement of it all. Anything could wait round the corner.

My company Mahon Digital Marketing is now on its 6th year, and since its humble beginnings, the company has grown into a flourishing international media agency with offices in London UK and Finland Scandinavia. Our 14-strong team keeps on driving the business forward, and I feel like my initial 'relationship' has developed into a fully-fledged family.

Starting out as a one-woman-operation back in 2010 was due to a fairly simple dream of mine; I wanted to practise digital marketing for my own clients, and I wanted to rule my own day around my young family's needs and as I saw convenient.

I never really thought of the concept of being 'an entrepreneur', or launching a 'startup'.

All I wanted to do was follow my passion and the rest seemed to follow as a natural cause.

Growth

Scaling up the company has been a (positive) challenge, and I've truly learned the ropes of being a leader of a growing business.

During growth, I've hired more people to drive the business forward, I've increased the company's service portfolio – and I've also been able to launch other companies to support the ecosystem around the business.

It's been almost six years of passion, and I hope many more to come. I feel that this is only the beginning and the building blocks are all falling into their correct places. I am very excited about the future and I hope to see many more ladies starting up their businesses too! Go for your passion, and do it today.

Christina Guidotti Bio

Christina Guidotti is one of Australia's leading experts on belief, conviction and commitment in areas of sales, leadership, productivity, achievement and fulfilment.

As an authentic, powerful and inspiring speaker, author, mentor and trusted professional advisor she partners with individuals, businesses and organisations to create life-changing and sustainable outcomes.

Leading Women

Christina Guidotti – Australia

I'm the kind of girl who has always gone for what she wants, heaps of belief, conviction and commitment, a serial True Believer. There's so much I am grateful for and like many there's been some successful failures along the way, lots of valuable life lessons. I've been climbing the ladder of success in business for over 25 years. I have always been successful in my industry, leading highly productive and profitable teams.

My real estate team achieved brilliant results winning industry awards and recognition, and the financial rewards were there. But being productive has always been a necessity. I was juggling so much, myself, family, friends, sellers, buyers, team and career, all while building and renovating several houses. It was hectic. I'd run all day long until I would often collapse into bed at night. As a working mum there was much hard work but the rewards were there.

Mastering productivity became a necessity as I wanted to have it all and I was determined. Saying no more to low value tasks and getting the right support were paramount. Many over the years have asked why I have so much stamina. Belief, conviction and commitment to having it all, both achievement and fulfilment, is what gives me stamina.

I want to:

- have my best health
- have my best relationships — family, friends and at work
- do work that I love
- have wealth to give freedom for the future
- live with peace and fulfilment.

And for over a decade in real estate I had a dream that I would own one of the best real estate brands in Australia. My energy, my driving force to this dream. For 10 years I kept this dream essentially to myself, just telling a few special others. I worked hard at it. And there was a lot of evidence coming through that I was on my way. After 10 years leading an award winning team, the problem still remained that I wasn't an owner in the company. Although I was accomplished as a leader, I wasn't the CEO, it wasn't my gig. But I kept on going and held in my heart a strong belief that one day I would be the owner.

Then after 10 years I decided it was time to share my ambition, I had nothing more to prove. It was time to not just be the leader but an owner in my life picture to own my own frame.

So I called the CEO of the company, my dad and invited him to lunch, you know, one of those special long business lunches, when you block out the rest of the afternoon. So I booked the finest restaurant, white table cloth and fancy menu and fine wines, for an afternoon that was to end in celebration. The day had finally arrived when I would declare my ambition. But in that moment I saw that my dream would not keep.

The reality was that it was time to stop dreaming this dream. Although many would say my life looked picture perfect, I was still living the wrong picture! I was living someone else's picture. That day I realised that this wasn't my legacy and that I had lost ownership of my frame.

And this was one of the greatest tipping point of my life, the pain woke me up to the truth I had been ignoring and forced me to make a few overdue decisions. The greatest lesson was to have the courage to live the life I chose and not live in someone else's frame.

Like all True Believers I persisted with:
1. Belief — hope, trust and resilience
2. Conviction — congruence, confidence and courage
3. Commitment decision, discipline and direction.

There have been many lessons from this experience but most of all:

- I will never not speak out again, never hide my ambition, never settle!
- I will always speak my truth, always declare my ambition, always live in my own frame!
- I will live my legacy helping other True Believers to create their own life masterpiece!

This type of story and this tipping point are so common. So many climb the ladder of success only to wake up one day to find they are not where they want to be. What we do next in these challenging times is crucial to our success. I made a decision not to be passive, not to settle – but to create my own life masterpiece, a life of purpose and fulfilment as a speaker, author and mentor helping to empower women to undress their ambition and to live as a True Believer.

"I never dreamed about success. I worked for it."
Estée Lauder

Jessica Cox Bio

As a person who has never viewed herself as a victim of her condition, Jessica shares in her speech humorous stories of struggle and success living in a "two-handed" world. She provides critical insight on how best to approach a challenge, redefining the concept of innovative thinking. She helps people reconnect with their own inner strengths and aptitudes.

Jessica believes in combining creativity, desire, persistence, and fearlessness; with them, nothing is impossible. In her presentation, she will dig deep into her experiences living armless in a two-handed world and share how these four elements helped her achieve the seemingly impossible.

Disarm Your Limits

Jessica Cox – USA

Jessica Cox is recognized internationally as an inspirational keynote speaker. Born without arms, Jessica now flies airplanes, drives cars, and otherwise lives a normal life using her feet as others use their hands. She holds the title of the first person without arms to get a black belt in ATA Martial Arts and the Guinness World Record for being the first armless person in aviation history to earn a pilot's certificate. Convinced that the way we think has a greater impact on our lives than our physical constraints, she chose to pursue a degree in psychology at the University of Arizona. Since then she has traveled to 20 countries and 6 continents sharing her inspirational message.

Born in 1983 in Sierra Vista, Arizona, Jessica has learned to live her life with her feet. There were many questions at the time about whether Jessica would be able to live a "normal" life. However, Jessica's father has said he never shed a tear about her birth condition. He had full confidence in her potential. With the support of her parents and family,

Jessica became confident in herself as an adult and continued to explore the world with her feet.

Jessica's parents met a Taekwondo instructor named Jim Cunningham. His response when told of Jessica's birth condition was that she would be more than physically able to participate and that only her attitude could hold her back. At the age of 14, Jessica earned her first black belt in the International Taekwondo Federation.

After graduating from high school, Jessica attended the University of Arizona where she earned a bachelor's degree in psychology. When talking about her degree, she frequently explains that psychology credits the way people think with having a greater impact on their lives than a physical limitation.

During college, Jessica joined an ATA Martial Arts club and resumed training in the sport of Taekwondo. Even though Jessica already had one black belt in a different style, she had to relearn all of the color belt material. The instructors created a standardized curriculum that would be accessible to any future armless students. Jessica then became the first armless person to earn a black belt in the ATA. Jessica is also a Certified Trainer in the ATA.

Jessica's most famous accomplishment was learning how to fly. It took three states, four airplanes, three flight instructors, and three years to find the right aircraft: a 1946 415C Ercoupe Airplane. In 2008 Jessica earned her Light Sport Pilot Certificate. She received the Guinness World Record for being the first person certified to fly an airplane with only their feet in 2011.

In May 2012, Jessica married in the beautiful city of South Pasadena, CA. In the fall of that same year, Jessica became a Goodwill Ambassador for Handicap International, a Nobel Peace Prize winning NGO and has advocated for disability rights in Ethiopia, Philippines and the US Senate.

Jessica is now the subject of an award winning documentary about her life. Right Footed features Jessica's journey from motivational speaker to mentor and international rights activist.

Have you ever felt like you didn't belong? Like everything was chaos around you, you didn't have the support you wish you had, and your motivation to keep going was slipping through your fingers? If this sounds familiar, then you know how it feels to be "disarmed." In Jessica's first book, she lays out the tools you need to design your own "formula for flight." You have the ability to turn the obstacles you face around and use them to your advantage. All you need is the formula for flight.

Are you ready to become the pilot in command of you?

"The only safe ship in a storm is leadership."
Faye Wattleton

Micaela Becattini Bio

With an International Career and first-hand experience of intense life changes, Dr. Micaela Becattini is an Igniter for solutions, "victim-free" attitude, self-expression and courage for people, who are undergoing life-transitions, change and life adversities.

Through her knowledge, practical guidance and experience, she provides her clients the tools to find new understandings and pathways through change and transformation.

Micaela serves her purpose of cultivating self-believe and strength in people by offering engaging and creative tools and workshops for finding the light in the midst of struggle in life.

Micaela passionately believes that harnessing the courage to reveal yourself enables people to get out of boxed mentality and live a life, which is true to who they are.

Graceful Life Transitions

Dr. Micaela Becattini – Australia

Today, my world is full of excitement, dreams, possibilities and action.

I can say that I am immersed in a new and flourishing existence. I follow the flow of life which is essential to finding my inner harmony. I try not to judge, to remain open to every possibility and say a full and unconditional YES to any situation life proposes me, learning to leave behind with love what has been and what is no longer.

But you see, my big life adventure didn't start like this. Ohhh nooo!

In July 2004 I decided to leave Italy and my home to follow my soul mate to Australia but didn't realise how much energy I had to consume to keep my love and my passion alive!

I remember the day when my trembling fingers wanted to hold onto not just the door of the airplane, but also everything I had ever known, my native language, my cultural traditions, my thriving practice, my family, my friends…my identity for 29 years that I was leaving behind.

For a long time, after my move, I felt capable and useless at the same time. Everyday felt like a long phase of burden with daily feelings of inadequacy. Life seemed like a giant void that nothing could fill. Anxiety was rife. Basic activities seemed like world shattering events, above all after being diagnosed with Crohn's Disease and Reactive Arthritis in October 2007.

All of this contributed to me developing patterns of a "victim behaviour". The biggest point was the feeling of not being understood, followed by wanting to be recognised, a lack of good judgement, people pleasing, committing to something that would never work just to get attention, blaming others and the surrounding situations.

I am glad that I had the knowledge and awareness to move through that phase. As a qualified therapist and coach, instead of staying stuck in that phase, I was able to change my story.

Slowly but surely, I started collecting courage, wisdom, help, my luck-making ideas and splintered on the path of growth re-creating my now successful business in 2012.

I knew that I had to surrender to the cycle of loss, I had to recognise the difficulties of the moment and accept that an initial transition period of confusion and sadness, was not only normal but also necessary to adapt to the new situation.

I sat down, grabbed some paper and a pen and started to re-write my personal and business needs, wants, desires and strengths followed by my new values as an evolved person. I then dedicated my time to identifying achievable goals and nurturing my new business ideas, comparing them to the surrounding new reality, being open to new possibilities, learning new ways to interact and when needed, outsourcing and asking for some help!

Now, I am a LIFE TRANSITION SPECIALIST and support whoever goes through intense personal and/or professional transitions. I help them master their mindset, understand their emotions and tap into their true resilience so they can move through trials and changes with more ease and grace without suffering a complete meltdown and leaving behind a "victim attitude".

Today I am on a mission to help "my people" arrive at the other side of transition with gumption and energy and guiding them towards their goals and dreams. I am here to show them that when they know what they want and they have the courage to go after it, their mind and emotions work as a team to help them accomplish their goals!

"One's philosophy is not best expressed in words; it is expressed in the choices one makes... and the choices we make are ultimately our responsibility."
Eleanor Roosevelt

Jacqui Kalka Bio

Jacqui Kalka is a Brand and Territory Owner at Mike Pero Real Estate. She started her real estate career in 2001 and Ian in 1981. Over that time they have both achieved many awards and accolades for outstanding achievement and results.

Now with over 50 years combined experience they are proud to combine their expertise and experience with the innovative Mike Pero Brand.

Life Can Change in an Instant

Jacqui Kalka – New Zealand

Life can change in an instant – it's what you take from the experience that teaches you the most.

On January 22nd 1991 my life changed in an instant.

At the time I had a job which worked well for my family. I worked part time in a Bank and had all the school holidays off. It was important to me that I was home with my two sons then aged 13 and 11.

I remember the day as if it was yesterday. It was a beautiful summer's day, the boys and I had been out for lunch and I had purchased their school uniforms for the coming school term.

We returned home and my youngest son decided to ask his friend over for a swim. I could hear them in the pool and they were having lots of fun. The next moment I ventured onto the deck to see my son in his friend's arms. He had died in the pool. I remember standing there as the paramedic delivered the news thinking to myself, "How does life change so quickly?". The effect on our family was profound. I don't believe his Dad ever recovered and in some ways, I believe he blamed himself. My oldest son lost his best friend and to this day it still leaves a huge void for him. He now has his own son and I know he must often wish his wee boy could have met his little brother.

Moving through this was one of the biggest challenges I had ever faced at that stage of my life. Eventually the days passed into weeks and then to years. That child is my "Peter Pan forever" as I still see him as 11 when in fact he would now be a young man.

As the years passed we decided to try for another child. At the time I was 41 so wasn't really confident that it would be easy. But it was. Within weeks I was pregnant with a beautiful daughter. She will celebrate her 21st this year – 2016.

My relationship with their Dad hadn't always run smoothly. I don't want to go into the story too deeply as I have moved on and now live a very joyous life filled with love, happiness and gratitude.

The relationship had always been abusive in a more subtle way. In May 2004 he physically attacked me early one morning and the police were called. He went into therapy and I decided to give it another try. It only lasted a month until I finally decided to leave for good. My daughter was 9 at the time and I now know it was the best thing to do for myself and my children.

I truly wish him well and send blessings and love his way every day. It would fill me with joy if he could move forward and enjoy what life has to offer.

I have remarried and am truly happy. Life is treating me well and my husband has been wonderful for my children. My daughter has blossomed into a beautiful young lady with his love and support.

It has served as a reminder to me that life throws lessons at you to teach you. I never knew being with a man could be this easy. He truly is my source of inspiration and our goal moving forward is to help others when and where we can. Your thoughts, your words and your actions are truly powerful!

> **Sara Redman Bio**
>
> Sara Redman is the Co-Director of SRA Corporate Change. SRA Corporate Change works with organisations and their leaders to unlock their potential and co-create high performance. Prior to her current role, Sara worked in an extensive range of positions, some of which fulfilled her, others of which did not. From these experiences, one key learning she has taken away is that understanding your strengths is the key to success.

Understanding Your Strengths is The Key to Success

Sara Redman – Australia

I am a mother, stepmother, partner, business owner, pilates instructor, daughter, sister, author, coach, friend and a semi-reformed control freak.

My current role is Co-Director of SRA Corporate Change. At SRA Corporate Change we work with organisations and their leaders to unlock their potential and co-create high performance.

I grew up in Toronto, Canada and moved to Australia when I was 25 years old. Sadly, my beautiful mother died of cancer when she was 46 and I was 7. Throughout my life, my mother has always been a major inspiration for me. She was an author of several healthy recipe books for families and had her own TV show on preparing healthy food. In the 70's this was ahead of her time, as the preference was packaged, convenience foods. I always remember baking bread with my Mom, picking veggies out of our home garden and making bran muffins, homemade yogurt and bircher muesli. I also remember her kindness, her energy, her intelligence and her ability to engage with people.

I studied at University of Toronto and completed an Honours Degree in Psychology. After graduating I was unable to find a job, and really wanted to come to Australia on a working visa. So I made the decision to move to Australia and fortunately, felt at home right away. I stayed with some friends I had met overseas, backpacked around the country, and then started to work in an employment and training company. I ended up working here for over a decade.

At this time of my life, I was absolutely fixated on climbing the corporate ladder thinking the higher I got the happier I would be. Sadly, I was sorely mistaken. When I became a Senior Executive I was ironically more unfulfilled at work than I had ever been. I felt removed from people and swamped with policy, papers, and procedures. It took me almost two years to muster up the courage to leave this very respectable role and venture into the unknown. Upon leaving the organisation, I was lucky that I was able to take a redundancy package that gave me a few months buffer to find my feet. Leaving this role was most definitely the best thing I could have done, but was extremely hard at the time. All of a sudden when people asked me 'what do you do?' I literally couldn't answer. I realised how much my identity had been connected to my job and my title, and I was a bit shocked and embarrassed by this. I carried out some soul searching to figure out who I really was, and what I really wanted in my life, not just professionally but personally too.

As a result of this reflection, I ended up working as a consultant in project management with businesses I had already known through my previous job. I also decided to become accredited in pilates, as my favourite pilates instructor (and the only one at the time in Launceston) was moving away. I enjoyed the consulting for a while, and I continue to enjoy running pilates classes today.

After reflecting more I realised that my strengths lie in communication, particularly – speaking, deeply listening, working one on one and in small groups, with an ability to draw people out, and always see, the good in people. Having worked as a counsellor I remembered my passion to support people and to help them realise their potential, and I decided to become accredited as a coach. Eventually I was able to weave this into my business, and I changed to straight consultancy, which included wellbeing coaching and corporate workshops. In hindsight this was a good move as today I deliver strategy, leadership, culture & wellbeing programs with our team of 10 at SRA Corporate Change.

I should mention this was all after several business attempts and failures. The failures were hard, but provided an immense amount of learning. For example, I learnt the importance of partnering with people who are aligned with your values and beliefs, of putting your working goals, plans and strategies in writing and ensuring you are on the same page, I learned how important it is to have the strength to back your gut instinct, because in my experience, it always seems to be right.

I experienced many crisis points in my life, as we all do, and only just learned recently that the Chinese characters for crisis are 'danger' and 'opportunity'. What an apt pairing! When we find the opportunity in the crisis it helps us let go, and move forward which to me is what resilience is all about.

Throughout my working life I have always had a deep desire to author a book. I feel this very likely links back to my Mother and her working life. I cannot say how many times I have planned or half written a book but never got them to a point of completion. Clearly something was blocking me. I had an insight when I found myself standing in the pantry one day, having an intense desire for chocolate. Now I don't normally have chocolate in the house but I was desperate so even considered cooking chocolate! Then I stopped and asked myself 'what is going on here?' In that moment I realised that I felt as if I wasn't enough to complete a book! Who was I to share my knowledge or experience with the world? It all came down to self doubt – something that I have seen time and time again in myself, in my family and friends, and in the 100's of clients I had coached at this point. So guess what? The insight meant I no longer wanted chocolate…and it helped me move forward to finally complete my first book. Glimpse is all about assisting you in catching a glimpse of the person you have the potential to become – your best possible YOU. We all can be that person, sadly, we just don't all see it… yet.

I am proud and inspired to have completed this book when I was 46 years old and my son was 7, which is the same age my Mom was when she died, and the age I was at the time.

My main message? Notice when you are doubting yourself and be gentle with yourself. This is normal but also a time to find the courage to push through. How do you do this? Really take the time to get to know your own unique strengths and talents. It is only when we know our strengths and bring them into our lives that we can find true fulfilment.

Jeany Park Bio

Jeany Park is the Owner of Compass Rose Video, a boutique videography agency that caters to small and medium sized businesses in the Portland, Oregon area.

Her background includes professional acting and she is passionate about helping to elevate the businesses and lives of women entrepreneurs through the power of Video.

How to be a SoloPreneur in 7 Steps

Jeany Park – USA

The low point was not finding myself unemployed at the age of 41 after having moved my family to a different state so that I could work at a prestigious classical theatre company. The low point was not that after switching from acting to life coaching that I had zero clients. No, the lowpoint was probably when I realized that I had spent the entire workday as an office administrator at a high tech company in Portland, Oregon, surfing the likes of TMZ, Perez Hilton and Buzzfeed…ALL DAY LONG!!! 8 hours of my life evaporated, and I had nothing to show for it but the $200 that I had made that day sitting at reception, that and an internet/surfing hangover after filling my head with the intellectual equivalent of Twinkies and Ho-ho's. Something had to give!

So I did it…I finally took the leap, quit my day job and decided to embark full time as a video marketing coach. Within 1 month I had booked 6 clients, within 3 months I had my whole business up & running including getting my business license, hiring my business coach, creating my own website and within 6 months, not only had I broken even, I had already grossed $12,000. I am happy to say that less than a year into my business, we are now financially stable and poised to hit 6 figures this calendar year. Life is good!

People ask me how I was able to make the transition, and to make my business successful – even at a somewhat modest level – in such a short amount of time. Here are the secrets to my success:

1. You have to go all in. If you half a** it, you won't be successful.
2. Start a morning ritual that jump starts your day with positivity and anchoring yourself with your goals – my favorite is the Miracle Morning – check out the book by Hal Elrod. It'll change your life.
3. Done is better than perfect – don't make the mistake of waiting until everything is perfect. Much better to learn on the go, just create something, anything, put it out there and wait and see.
4. Get a coach! Or mentor! You can't do it alone and you'll save yourself SO much time. Derive benefit from someone who's done it before you.
5. Stop being a frickin' people pleaser! You're going to have to say no to things – like volunteering, flake out once in awhile on commitments you've already made, let other people be the good soldier. For the 1st 3 months you have to be super selfish and focus on your new business. Think of it like having a newborn baby – you won't sleep much, you'll drop off the face of the planet, forget exercise and things like showering, but soon – very soon, it will all be worth it.
6. Trust your instincts! If it doesn't feel right, don't do it. You know better than anyone. Full stop!
7. Ask your community what they want from you? What's the pain point? Then figure out how you're going to solve it.

Okay, I lied – here's 8):...

8. Use video – really, it works! I built a career on it, that's how much faith I have in it. Video + social media is a 1-2 punch that's unstoppable.

The moral of my story is don't wait until it's too late. Life is short, take the leap! What you'll learn about yourself is the reward in itself, 10x over.

Kate Worsfold Bio

Kate is the CEO and Founder of Wings of Destiny. She proudly lives in the city of Ipswich, QLD and is a wife, and a mother to five beautiful children with ages ranging from 21 to 4 years old. She runs her business full time, is a passionate community advocate and devotes her heart to building others up that have suffered trauma and pain in their life.

She is committed to helping every woman, man and child reconnect themselves to their authentic self and teaches them that their self-confidence, self-belief, happiness and wholeness is the elixir to their life.

Empowering Women to Become the Masters of Their Own Destiny Post Domestic Violence

Kate Worsfold – Australia

I am a survivor of 15 years of Domestic Violence wanting to share my story with as many people as I can to help bring an awareness of this insidious and evil social ill. After spending my career in Managerial and Operational roles in various small business and corporate companies, I was given the privilege of working for the *Queensland Times Newspaper* as their Adopt a Family Appeal Coordinator.

During my time working with so many underprivileged people within the community, I realised my passion was to help those who needed to find their wings and their voices, especially those who had suffered like me at the hands of Domestic Violence (DV) abusers. I then forged my organisation *Wings of Destiny* focusing on assisting women who have left DV relationships, to find their self-empowerment, self-confidence and freedom again and empower them to never return to relationships of abuse.

I understand all too well the paradox in leaving a DV relationship and then revoking the decision to retreat and return. One of the prevalent reasons I believe most women return to these relationships is because these women lack clarity in their self-identity and confidence. I believe they lose who they are and become conditioned into believing what others think of them, consumed by their limitations instead of focused on their true potential and the greatness they have within them.

I am committed to helping women be reunited with their true selves and finding their wings to fly so that they are capable of forging an amazing destiny for themselves that is not comprised by abuse. I have written a 6 week program "Destined to be ... ME" that takes women on a deep soulful journey on finding their inner values, bringing them in alignment back with their authentic and true sense of self and learning how not to allow their negative experiences and trauma to define who they are but rather they learn the tools on how to define themselves based on their personal victories and greatness they already possess deep down inside.

I am a strong community advocate in helping women and families post DV and I facilitate my course through various community centres in the region with the sponsorship of various businesses helping to subsidise placements for these women to rebuild their lives and additionally through the endorsement of several community campaigners and MP's. I have also written a book which is due to be published.

Carmen Harrison & Cassandra Rathgeber Bio

Carmen Harrison and Cassandra Rathgeber are strong women, mothers, wives, sisters, dreamers and owners of Queen Bees Food Truck. Together we designed and created our dream Food Truck servicing Central Alberta, Canada.

We, Carmen and Cassandra hope to inspire everyday women, mothers, or anyone with a dream or passion. We hope to encourage you to never give up and to understand that if it feels right in your heart then it is of course anything is possible! Never allow people to shy you away from your true passion and what makes you happy.

Anything is Possible

Carmen Harrison and Cassandra Rathgeber – Canada

If someone told my sister and I that 2 years ago we would be young entrepreneurs running our very own food truck, we would have never believed them. We are twins from a farm with big dreams and aspirations, and our passion is food. We absolutely love to bake. It puts us in a relaxed and comfortable zone, a place where you can think, dream and be true to who you really are. Our goal when starting our food truck was to connect to our community through our food. We wanted to create an experience that everyone could enjoy. In the past year, we are so proud to say we have created our passion; Queen Bees Food Truck.

Queen Bees did not happen over night... It felt like it took a lifetime for the vision to arrive in our lives. Following college and without a clear idea of a concrete career path, both Cassandra and I had worked jobs in the hospitality industry. These jobs helped build the work ethic we would need to start Queen Bees. We both married young and decided to stay at home and run a dayhome. This allowed us stay at home and raise our children. After several years had passed we found ourselves in a place of uncertainty. We were internally struggling with a direction to take in our lives. We both new this wasn't our true path or purpose.

In the evening, we would walk and on these walks the seeds of the Queen Bees idea began to grow. We started to create our vision, discuss ideas, argue details and slowly the dream took shape. We made vision boards to help us manifest our reality. As time went on we felt we were getting closer to actualizing our plan but our 5 children were still really young, between 18 months to 4 years old. That was our major hurdle, trying to balance our children and a full-time job. But honestly, we needed a change in our lives. It wasn't healthy for our well being and we wanted to show our children how to reach for the stars. We felt we owed it to ourselves to follow our dreams, and to show our children if you believe in yourself, anything is possible. Many people have faced hard challenges and even impossible ones and still found success. We were also nervous of the one thing all entrepreneurs are scared of…failure. Yet, because of our prior experiences, our bond with each other, and the belief we could succeed, failure was tempered by excitement. We knew this adventure was about our personal growth and about discovering who we really are as people.

This idea kept blossoming. We created the menu in 2 minutes. It was basically all our favourite treats. However, we did teach ourselves to make French Macarons. We loved them, and thought it would be a treat to share with our community. We purchased an old delivery truck online that had no engine. We had no idea how this was going to come to life. Our childhood neighbour came to our rescue and made this entire truck a reality for us. We couldn't believe our luck. Len Aucoin was able to transform this shell of a truck in to a beautiful full service Food Truck.

After one season in the books and many lessons learned, Queen Bees Food Truck is nearly booked solid for the 2017 season. We service the City of Red Deer as well as Sylvan Lake and surrounding areas. We are so excited to see where Queens Bees takes us. We are still dreaming big and hope to open a store front in the near future. We have endless ideas and it will always be in our nature to reach for the stars.

Zoë Routh Bio

Zoë Routh is a leadership expert who has worked with individuals teams internationally and in Australia since 1987. She is passionate about helping leaders and teams thrive together, especially through times of volatile change. She believes that connectivity in teams, combined with change literacy, will create business resilience. She knows that when we speak our truth, we lead and elevate all.

Her past leadership roles include Chair of the Outdoor Council of Australia and President of the ACT Chamber of Women in Business.

She is the author of Composure: How centered leaders make the biggest impact. Her forthcoming book is Speak Your Truth: Leadership In Moments That Matter Most.

Zoë is an outdoor adventurist and enjoys telemark skiing, has run 6 marathons, is a one-time belly-dancer, and loves hiking in the high country. She is married to a gorgeous Aussie and is mother to 6 garden-wrecking chooks.

Discovering Your Inner Compass

Zoë Routh – Australia

I'm a British-born, Canadian raised, Australian adventurist. I came out of the womb ready to explore the world! My mother used to have to tie me around the waist with a rope to keep me from wandering off. That sense of adventure has stayed with me always.

My first real job was leading canoe trips across Northwest Ontario. It was wild, rugged and spectacular. I learned that the world is truly beautiful. I also learnt the value of companionship and the strength that comes with a tightly knit group. Belonging and connection are the heart's currency.

From there I ventured across the continent and another ocean to land in Australia and work with Outward Bound Australia. For the next 10 years I had amazing adventures in remote parts of Australia, down its wild rivers, up its stunning mountains. I learned about leadership of my colleagues and how to set the direction for an organisation with limited resources. Here I established the registered training organisation and set up the Internship program, a year-long outdoor instructor development program. With my team I taught new outdoor leaders the technical and interpersonal skills required to help people develop themselves in remote settings. This included canoeing, rafting, abseiling, bushwalking, and high ropes courses, as well as facilitation and debriefing.

In 2005 after I'd launched my leadership development business Inner Compass, I discovered I had cervical cancer. It was not the usual kind and it was very aggressive. This was the news I received one week after getting engaged to my gorgeous Aussie man. We were devastated. Our plans for wedding and babies turned upside down.

I put my business on hold and underwent several months of chemotherapy and extensive abdominal surgery. These were dark days. Once I recovered, we underwent years of IVF, with roadblock after roadblock in our way. In 2010, we closed the door on that future, and embraced one without children. This has been both heart-wrenching and rewarding. We count our life as blessed.

I decided to live my life differently as a result and began a new adventure. For the next few years I reinvented myself, explored new ways of running my business and then landed a job with the Australian Rural Leadership Foundation. Here I continued to have my wild adventures as the ARLF included outdoor experiential learning with its programs. I developed leadership programs for various industry sectors like wine, rice, and mining communities. It was glorious!

The call for my own business kept pulling me back. In 2014 I embraced my leadership practice once more and it has been widely successful. I am deeply passionate about helping leaders discover the power of their voice and speaking their truth. I believe that leaders who develop themselves contribute in big ways to the planet. I am honoured to work with a number of CEOs and organisations as they hone their leadership, thinking, being and doing in service to better industries and communities.

The key insights for me are to keep the adventurist spirit alive, even through dark areas of life. To keep exploring, being curious, and savouring the views is my inner compass that guides me through life's adventures.

"I always thought that people told you that you're beautiful–that this was a title that was bestowed upon you…I think that it's time to take this power into our own hands and to say, You know what? I'm beautiful. I just am. And that's my light. I'm just a beautiful woman."
Margaret Cho

Sue Stockdale Bio

Sue Stockdale is a sought-after motivational speaker and coach who inspires business leaders around the world to achieve exceptional performance. She has a detailed understanding of motivation and leadership, gleaned from her experience in business, adventure and sport.

In 1996, she became the first UK Woman to ski to the Magnetic North Pole and she has represented Scotland in track and field athletics. Her career included a senior management role in a UK utility, and a period with the United Nations working in a war zone. Sue's presentations are delivered with passion and energy, so that people leave feeling they can achieve things they did not imagine were possible.

Stepping Into the Unknown Can Be Worthwhile

Sue Stockdale – UK

As a young girl, growing up in Scotland, I used to love reading adventure stories about ordinary people who had achieved extraordinary things. Some were fictional, like Enid Blyton's Famous Five, and others were real-life adventurers like Edmund Hillary, and Ernest Shackleton. Reading these stories made me want to become an adventurer – but I began to believe that to do so, you had to be a man, or have a lot of money. It was not until many years later, that these limiting beliefs were challenged, and in 1996, I became the first British woman to reach the Magnetic North Pole. I realised that we can all achieve amazing things, but often the only person stopping you…..is you.

Taking a risk

My career began at 16 years old, and like many people it was in an office role in British Gas. Whilst in the company, I was keen to progress, and during my 11-year career I held various roles including within the Corporate Training function, and became one of the youngest employees to reach a Senior Management role. However, I still had an adventurous mindset, so eventually decided to leave that cosy corporate lifestyle behind, and embark on a 1-year contract in a war zone working for the United Nations! That seemed like a big risk to me, but a great opportunity at the same time, to work in an international setting, and learn how the culture and politics operate within large governmental organisations. It was a huge change and it took me some time to adapt, but what I learned that was most useful was about risk taking. When you are prepared to step into the unknown, it can be scary, but you can learn a lot. It means when the next big risk comes along you are much better prepared for it.

The big opportunity

One year later I was back home reading the newspaper, when an advert got my attention. It said "wanted 10 novice arctic explorers to trek to the Magnetic North Pole". I did not even know where that was, but it sounded cold! Over 500 people applied for the expedition, and eventually I was selected to join the team, led by David Hempleman-Adams. And, after a 30-day journey in temperatures cold enough to freeze your flesh in seconds, we achieved our goal – it was a great feeling of achievement! This experience then inspired me to go on more adventures and I went on to Antarctica, Greenland, and the Geographical North Pole. All of these expeditions taught me the realities of risk-taking, leadership, managing change and maintaining motivation, which I help business leaders put into practice today.

The adventure of building a business

I decided to use these lessons, plus my business and training experience and in 1997 I founded a company that helped women to start up and grow businesses. By building a strong brand reputation, we grew the business and in 2007 I faced a tough decision. Do I grow the business, find a Managing Director to run it, sell it, or close it? I realised that my passion lay in working directly with clients and inspiring them, rather than being a business leader, so I decided to sell the company to focus on utilising my core strengths of inspiring others.

Today I integrate my unique combination of business acumen, adventure experience and leadership capabilities in my work. Sometimes its individual coaching, delivering a motivational presentation to a team, or a leadership programme for an organisation. My clients are varied, from corporate leaders to people in elite sport as well as not for profit organisations and small businesses. They are based around the world, but all want to be able to achieve exceptional performance. I don't think the journey of growth ever ends, we all need to keep on stepping into the unknown to explore what we are capable of.

"To be beautiful means to be yourself. You don't need to be accepted by others. You need to accept yourself."
Thich Nhat Hanh

Ruby Usman Bio

Ruby Usman is an Author, Speaker and Educator. With a brilliant business mind, an international career and first-hand experience of the hardships of life, she is an inspiring adventurer.

Ruby is the founder of Healing Wounds Together, which is an excellent resource for not only those who are affected by childhood sexual abuse but also professionals who work with them. Ruby is creator of 'Self Care Method', which is pathway for creating sustainable collective happiness. The method is delivered through three essential pillars: self, family & relationships, and community. Ruby has also authored a book 'Self Care for Parents' – A 5-step method to having a happy balance in life.

Finding Freedom Within
Ruby Usman – Australia

Having grown up in the slums of Pakistan, I was conditioned by the culture to think of myself as a "non-being" – someone whose pleasure and goals weren't important. I saw men beat their women (sisters, wives and other family members); children were yelled at and abused and I was myself sexually abused as a child for many years.

Luckily, my parents weren't following the cultural norms so despite these cultural conditions, I was able to study and even get myself a job in a multinational firm. It was almost like living in several worlds at the same time. Inside my own home, we were taught equality, respect and the value of good education. Outside my home, I was a slut because I didn't follow norms and didn't wear hijab. And inside my workplace, I was a confident woman surrounded by people who were educated and respectful of my worth and skills.

It was a strange world. Being aggressive was the prerequisite for me to stand firm in a world dominated by men.

In 1997, I got married with the dreams of love, respect and a life of harmony. Sadly, it didn't turn out that way. My married life was dominated by unconscious cruelty, painful sex, illnesses and a visit to a hospital. The cultural norms made it very hard for me to leave that marriage. I felt stuck and had nowhere to go. The only place of reprieve for me was the roof of the house where I hid away from time to time and cried.

My freedom came in the form of a job opportunity in Singapore. I left Pakistan in June 2000. This also gave me a pathway to finally leave the marriage. We got divorced in July 2002.

I was finally free (at least physically) but for the first time, I was out in the world on my own and I had no idea where to start. I used to have panic attacks. I remember crying on streets because I didn't want to go and sleep in a room by myself. Those were scary times.

I also realised that freedom was a state of mind. I was free at face value but I was still limited by my beliefs and my cultural conditioning. I had suppressed my desires and my needs for years and years and even now, when I was a free woman, my own limitation didn't allow myself to feel this freedom.

Finding freedom became a journey of exploration. I needed to know who I was and what I wanted but fundamentally, I needed to give myself permission to have needs and desires. I had no idea how to do that. I was in a strange country, didn't have many friends, didn't know the western customs and traditions; it felt like I had to learn to walk all over again, undo the brainwashing and reprogram myself to have new neural pathways.

This meant saying "Yes" to anything and everything that came my way. Life experiences became my teachers; and I started collecting my experiences; learning from my mistakes and from my own explorations. I missed having role models. I missed having someone who I could ask. I missed having support and assurance and safety. But that wasn't my path.

These explorations enabled me to live in four different cities and create a completely different life in each of these cities. My biggest learning experiences in Karachi, Pakistan; basics of western life in Singapore; fun and adventure in Sydney; love and relating in Melbourne. At the same time, my own personal healing journey took me deep into the world of conscious and unconscious mind, body and its relationship with the mind, and emotions and feelings and their impact on body and mind.

And my biggest learning is this we can't do it alone, we need love, and we need belonging.

So in Nov 2016, I have launched an online forum called *Healing Wounds Together* – A Platform for Adults who have experienced Childhood Sexual Abuse.

My life has been deeply impacted by these experiences. At times, I wondered if there were other people who felt the same? Was I the only one feeling these feelings of shame, hatred, anger, and self-pity? It took me a while to realise that I wasn't.

This blogging platform is my attempt to bring us together; to "be there" for each other; to understand that we not alone and there are millions of adults (if not billions) who are affected by this and feel a lot of those things that we do.

My aim is to share the following:

- My understanding of trauma and how it impacts us.
- How did I start my healing journey and how has it changed my life?
- I will give you information about various healing modalities that are out there that can help you heal.
- I intend to interview adults who have experienced childhood sexual abuse and share their journeys with you.
- I intend to interview various therapists and professionals who have impacted me deeply in my healing journey.

It is a scary world. I feel exposed and vulnerable but I also know that this vulnerability is critical for the change to occur.

"Life's surprises – Notice and cherish life's surprises. Just because it's not what you were expecting, doesn't mean it's not everything you've been waiting for. So take a deep breath when you're rejected from something good. It often means you're being redirected to something better. Be patient. Be positive. Keep going."

Anon

Allie Pasag Bio

Maritess Pasag, also known as "Allie" by her clients is a successful Entrepreneur who is passionate about providing a variety of professional assistance in customer service, data entry, management, virtual assistance, technical support, client relations, quality assurance, and training.

During her career, she has assisted the real estate industry with virtual assistance and other administrative needs. Prior her stint as an Online Service Provider, Allie worked as an agent in the Call Center Industry and has received numerous Commendations due to her Exemplary Customer Service.

I am known in the business world as "Allie"

Maritess Pasag – Philippines

I am Maritess. Family and friends call me "Tisya", but I am known in the business world as "Allie" I grew up in a loving family. I was a typical daddy's girl with simple dreams. I was raised by a hardworking home service beautician mother and a hardworking father who was a simple employee in an organization.

Those jobs meant having to make ends meet for them to provide for me and my brother. Being raised in that economic situation was a challenge for all of us: I wanted to raise our standard of living, I want to provide the best. Good thing I had a scholarship growing up. I was always at the top of the class and I even earned an engineering scholarship from the Philippine's premier university.

Then I met a boy who was exactly my opposite. He was the ideal guy every girl wanted, and I really fell for him. It was a relationship that our parents knew about and approved of. They trusted us but our curiosity and the promise of young love got ahold of us. I got pregnant during college and had to drop out of school because we already had to prioritise our family.

Coursing through Challenges

It was never easy. Not only was our life difficult but finding a job when you have not finished college in the Philippines meant that there are only a few opportunities. I had to settle for an outsourcing job as a call centre agent. I had to travel 2 to 3 hours to and from work everyday just to go to a graveyard shift job. It meant that I had to be away from my children at night just to provide for them. Although my husband had a stable job at that time, there were a lot of days when I skipped eating lunch because I wanted to save most of the money for my family.

My Candle fades

As if I had enough challenges, one of the greatest was surviving the passing away of my father. I may have mentioned that I was a daddy's girl. Indeed, I was, even when I was already married. My father would even pick me up from the bus station when I go home late from work. He was the greatest dad, and his passing was the worst time of my life. I wasn't even able to say goodbye to him as I was confined in the hospital when he passed away. I was devastated.

The challenge that gave me a chance to champion

I was almost dead sick. Working in graveyard shift job got the best of my health. I was always literally hospitalised because my health was suffering. I had to make a decision to leave my job once and for all. I tried looking for home-based jobs but was always scammed in the beginning. Until I was hired to become a virtual assistant, and that boss of mine even partnered with me. It was a good partnership. But good things never last, they say, our partnership had to end.

Being a champion meant losing some along the way

When my business partnership ended, I took the courage and established my own business. It was never easy as there were times that a client would retrieve their contract but I still had to extend my employee's salary. I didn't always win.

Championing for my family

After several years of challenges, now, I could say that I was able to overcome them with perseverance and the support of my family. I now own a Business Process Outsourcing company, earning over twenty times more than an average Filipino family does. We were able to build our own two-storey house which eventually became our office and now we are building our own home. We were able to purchase our own SUV which was only just a dream. Life is great and when I see pictures of our house in the past, I cannot help but be grateful. Challenges are part of our lives, and we can always champion them.

"It is only when we truly know and understand that we have a limited time on Earth and that we have no way of knowing when our time is up that we will begin to live each day to the fullest, as if it were the only one we had."
Elisabeth Kubler-Ross

> ### Dr Sherylle Calder Bio
>
> Dr Calder is regarded as the leading specialist in the field of visual skills and performance both in South African and international sport. She is the only person who holds a formal PhD in Visual Performance Skills Training.

Keep Your Eye on the Ball

Dr. Sherylle Calder – South Africa

Dr. Sherylle Calder was born in Bloemfontein, South Africa. Being an athlete from a young age participating mainly in ball sports, she played her first competitive field hockey match at the age of eight. As a result she soon began to become aware of how large a role her visual and perceptual skills played in her skilled performances. As she developed into an elite hockey player, she further developed her interest in the visual concepts of elite sport. From an early age she was never given any coaching instruction regarding vision and its possible role in the visually demanding game of hockey.

The sole advice received was the traditional admonitions of most coaches of 'keep your eye on the ball'. She however experienced, and even more so at an international level, that her visual and perceptual system was 'different' to others and perceived that it was an important part of performance at an elite level.

It all started one day, while she was playing alongside a girl whose father watched all their games and was a member of the Olympic qualifying committee. She was told that she was the only international hockey player he had ever seen who did not run on the field. He was amazed of her ability to sense opponents as if she had eyes in the back of her head.

It was then that she realised that there might be something there. She analysed the things she did and began to work out how to put them into a training programme. That is where it all started. She had to prove it and fortunately, she did.

After she completed her schooling and her first degree at the University of the Orange Free State, she studied for her Masters' degree at the University of Stellenbosch before registering for her Sport Science PhD under Prof Tim Noakes at the University of Cape Town. Between 1982 and 1996, she represented South Africa at Field and Indoor hockey, gaining 50 international caps since 1992. Recognition as one of the top players of her era came in 1995 when she was selected to the team comprising the top 11 players in the pre-Olympic Qualifying Hockey Tournament. Countries participating at this Tournament included Germany, Netherlands, Korea, China, Great Britain, Argentina and Canada. In 1996 she was selected for a World Invitation Select Team to help prepare the Australian Women's hockey team for the Atlanta Olympic Games.

Her Doctoral thesis grew out of her interests in understanding the training methods and game concepts used internationally in field hockey and, especially, the role that visual skills play in the improvement of sporting performance. She developed novel visual skills training programme to enhance the capacity of players to access performance-relevant visual information during play. Her studies established that the enhancement of visual skills, using these specific training programmes, measurably improved the on-field performance of hockey players. This effect was substantially greater than any achieved by conventional coaching and training programmes.

Currently, Dr. Calder is associated with the South African Sports Science Institute at Cape Town doing what she loves to do. She has always made sure she offers quality service, and high tech programme, EyeGym has long been recognised by the top sportsmen and women in the world, from All Black, Springbok and England rugby men, to leading other sporting teams all over the world.

Kate Toon Bio

Kate Toon is an award-winning SEO copywriter and SEO consultant with almost two decades of experience in all things advertising, digital and writing. She is originally from the UK but is now based just outside Sydney.

She has worked with big brands such as eHarmony, Curash and Kmart, and she's helped countless small businesses produce great content and improve their copywriting and SEO.

Kate is also the founder of *"The Clever Copywriting School"*, *"The Recipe for SEO Success eCourse"* as well as co-host on the Hot Copy Podcast.

She presents the *'Write for Business'* show for the Dale Beaumont's Business Blueprint channel.

I made Google love me

Kate Toon – Australia

I'd been working in advertising for nearly two decades in some of the biggest ad agencies (think Ogilvy and the like). But as I climbed each rung of the career ladder, I enjoyed my life less and less. There were days when I found myself sobbing on the way to work, or sneaking off to the loo to silently scream. I was not a happy monkey.

My husband worked for himself, and I was jealous of the freedom it afforded him. But as I was the breadwinner, I was doubtful whether we'd survive if both of us took the 'entrepreneur' route.

But then, around seven years ago, I happily found myself 'with child', I realised I could either stay in the agency world and never see my son, or give it all up.

It was an easy decision: I decided to go it alone.

But then, as contractor, I suddenly found myself five months pregnant, out of a job and with no maternity leave pay.

My plan was to set myself up as a copywriter.

I built myself a little WordPress website and waited for the work to flood in. There was just one problem, or rather about 20,000 of them: when I typed 'copywriter' into Google, oodles and oodles of other copywriters appeared.

I needed to work out how to make my website appear at the top of the rankings and I needed to work it out fast. The only way to do this was to get my head around the dark art of Search Engine Optimisation. So I did. I trained myself, experimented, built websites, made mistakes, and slowly my expertise grew. I did this with little or no budget and no outside help (SEO training courses were few and far between back then). I also did this while a sleep-deprived mum with a brand new baby to care for, a dog to walk, a house to clean, meals to cook, and a husband to occasionally grunt at.

I am now in the first three results on Google for hundreds of different keywords. Thanks to my SEO success, I've built a further two businesses – a copywriting school, and an eCourse teaching others how to achieve the same results. And yes, my eCourse just broke through the mythical six-figure barrier.

Since starting out in 2009, I've helped major corporates and many small businesses win the SEO war. I've written SEO-friendly copy, created engaging content, technically audited a few hundred websites, and run heaps of training workshops. I've survived website hacks, negative reviews from competitors, algorithm updates, writer's block, negative SEO campaigns and much more.

I've managed to tame the Google beast and make it love me and my website. It's been hard work, and it's a never-ending journey (SEO is for life not just for Christmas), but it's also hugely rewarding, and I'm so glad I was brave enough to take the plunge.

Ndidi Nwuneli Bio

Ndidi Okonkwo Nwuneli is a social entrepreneur with about two decades experience in International Development and Business Management working with multinational firms, the public sector, and international organizations.

Ndidi founded LEAP Africa, a nonprofit organization that focuses on encouraging leadership and development initiatives for youth and business owners in Nigeria.

Ndidi is also a co-founder of AACE Food Processing & Distribution Ltd. (AACE Foods)an indigenous agro-processing company in Lagos, Nigeria and one of the directors of Sahel Capital & Advisory Partners, an advisory and private equity firm in Nigeria, which focuses on the agribusiness and manufacturing sectors.

An Advocate and Champion for Other Women

Ndidi Nwuneli – Nigeria

I was born and raised in Enugu to the family of Professor Paul and Professor Rina Okonkwo. My parents, who are professors and worked at the University of Nigeria Enugu Campus were extremely devoted to raising children who were hard working, disciplined and ethical. My parents and my two older sisters were my earliest role models and continue to inspire and challenge me today! My parents exposed my siblings and I to the concepts of patriotism and service from very young ages. Despite their Ivy League education, they both chose to devote their lives to teaching in the Nigerian higher educational system, fighting against all odds to ensure some level of excellence in their respective departments.

Beyond the extremely supportive family and community in which I was raised, a defining moment for me as a child were my early encounter with Christ. I was invited to church by amazing university students who would visit the staff quarters periodically to invite children to Sunday school. Through their life's example and wonderful encouragement, I was drawn to the church and gave my life to Christ when I was thirteen years old.

I do not think that I have had any experience that I will characterize as the worst moment. However, some of my earliest memories of Children's' Day celebrations were speeches which informed us that we are leaders of tomorrow. However, I quickly realized the older many of these individuals who told us that we were leaders of tomorrow had no plans of stepping aside for others to lead. I also recognized that some of the individuals who have shaped our world started leading in their youth. This is primarily because it is when you are young that you have the most energy, time, creativity, and are willing to take risks. You see possibilities and not hindered by years of experience that often limits vision, and compels people to see obstacles instead of possibilities. In addition, with the average life expectancy of a Nigerian at 57 years, what does tomorrow hold for a young person who may not be live to see that future? This realization led me to establish LEAP to inspire, empower and equip young people to lead today and tomorrow!

The A-HA moment actually occurred during a trip to Venezuela with my husband's Harvard MBA class. During a bus trip to a rural community I was struck by the good roads, electricity, absence of police checkpoints and lamented about the disparity between Africa and many other world regions. The words Leadership, Effectiveness, Accountability and Professionalism, immediately sprung in my mind. I believed that if we could infuse these four traits into the lives of our people, especially our youth and entrepreneurs, we could transform our communities and countries in Africa.

I would like to encourage young women to recognize three things:

First to be recognized as an equal in the workplace, and to receive your fair share of the income and profits that you generate, manage your time and resources effectively. You must put in your best and ensure that your voice is heard, loud and clear. You must never use your role as a wife, mother, sister, or daughter, as an excuse for underperformance. Invest in lifelong learning, always upgrading your skills and surrounding yourself with at least three critical people – a mentor, a champion and a critic. A champion serves as your biggest cheerleader, encouraging you to dream big and achieve results. A critic tells you the truth about your shortcomings and provides constructive feedback. A mentor shows you what is possible through their life example.

Second, women are natural givers. Giving opens your heart to the needs of the world and also takes your eyes off your own lack. However, you also have to be prepared to ask for help when you need it, especially as you embark on the journey of marriage and motherhood. Your vulnerability makes you human and does not detract in any way from your self-worth.

Third, as you rise in your profession or industry, leave the door open for other women to enter. Be the first woman president, CEO, leader of an organization, but never the last one. Ensure that you are mentoring and grooming other women to take over from you. Fight against the stereotype that women do not support other women. Instead be recognized as an individual who supports others. Madeleine Albright has a quote which I love – "There is a special place in hell for women do not support other women!" I know you want to go to heaven…so start today to serve as an advocate and champion for other women.

"I love to see a young girl go out and grab the world by the lapels. Life's a bitch. You've got to go out and kick ass."
Maya Angelou

Dina Cooper Bio

Dina Cooper loves supporting people to be genuinely happy. Because when people are happy, they naturally want to help others be happy and THAT'S EXCITING! Her work helps Change Makers, who are parents and non-parents, create a platform within themselves to launch life head on from the inside-out. The proven results are happier people that want to connect and thrive.

Change Maker

Dina Cooper – Australia

I grew up with racism prevalent at my primary school. Being an Indian girl in a predominantly Anglo school, along with a few of my peers who were also subject to racism, I questioned my worth as a person. But only momentarily... I realised early on that deep down I knew I was an equal. It didn't matter that I had different colour skin, or I was female, or I didn't have as much money as others.

I knew this, but I didn't always display my equality on the outside. I would always try harder, be better, strive further so I would be accepted and what I didn't realise back then, that I know profoundly today, is that the only person that needs to accept me, is ME.

Today I love working with Change Makers. Helping them to build platforms within themselves to launch their missions and make the change they wish to see in the world, in a balanced, healthy and congruent way. The reality is for any of us who want to make change happen in our world, it has to come from a place of passion and practicality combined, for it to be sustainable...

Burnt out change makers only get so far – I know this from my own personal experience!

Equality is also something I love supporting people with. Whether it's at home, in the workplace, in relationships, in life.

The equality work that underlies all things I'm involved in, ties into the way that I work with change makers. Because when we feel equal we become equal. Because when we believe we can make change happen, we can create change. I want every person I know to follow their dreams and make it a practical reality.

I changed careers at the age of 35. My kids were then 2 and 4.

One day when I was churning through my work as a Chartered Accountant, I finally acknowledged the dull ache in my chest. The ache that said this wasn't enough and I couldn't imagine doing it for a moment longer.

I quit my job and went full on into a coaching career. I am so grateful I had support to do this. I studied, I qualified and have practiced every day since. It is no longer work, it is me expressing me – ALL of me.

Today I work with a combination of parents and nonparent Change Makers. The reason why I love working with parents is because they are raising our future generation. They have the greatest influence in creating change for our tomorrow, individually and collectively. When I can work with them, I get to work with our future generation and that is exciting!!!!

For me, creating change is all about balance. It's about how can I help and how can I be helped. How I can live a full life and support others to live their full life. How can I look after my own family, whilst supporting others to look after theirs.

There is not one balance that suits everyone, despite the myth. I believe balance is a unique assessment of what works for you, in your life. When you find or are supported to find your balance, life really flies!

If I had one wish for everyone, it is to believe that you are worthy and equal, to create anything you can dream of. And it is to know there is a reality to this. It does require perseverance, courage, strength, determination and it doesn't happen overnight, but it does happen. And it will happen if you start and then keep growing and going!

> ### Mandie Spooner Bio
>
> Mandie Spooner is a Nutritional Therapist and the owner of Viva Health and Wealth. She works with science-based questionnaires and advanced tools to pinpoint the unique needs of each individual and to build a personalised program that works.

Viva Health and Wealth

Mandie Spooner – Australia

Hi, I'm Mandie Spooner, I'm a mother, a wife and a nutritional therapist. I run my own growing business and keep our busy home on track, which is full of rowdy growing boys and one quieter grown man. None of that makes me particularly unique in any way, there are many thousands of women just like me, balancing all the elements in our lives.

In my previous life I was a graphic designer. I had my own successful business which allowed me to work round my family, but my passion for design was falling short and frustration was creeping in.

After feeling exhausted for longer than I felt was good for anyone, I thought there had to be a better way and unexpectedly discovered what great nutrition can do for you. I started a nutritional cleanse in February 2014 and, with no exaggeration, had life changing results from it. This prompted me to look more into nutrition and inspire others to make a positive change in their lives too.

I did this with the creation of a new business, Viva Health and Wealth and beginning my studies in nutrition.

I now work hard to help others understand how important nutrition is to their mental and physical wellbeing. My business offers nutritional solutions to people and supports them through the often life changing aspects that eating a great diet can have.

I have so many happy clients now that all the hard work of changing career and starting from scratch in an industry I knew nothing about to begin with has been totally worthwhile.

I now have a career I am passionate about, take care of my clients and it fits into my busy lifestyle. As well as taking care of my family and running my business, I can fit in, exercise and healthy living into my daily life, which had been lacking before.

I strongly believe we are responsible for everything in our lives and that everything happens for a reason, the good and the bad. I am grateful that I listened to my inner voice when it shouted at me to go out on a limb and try this new endeavor and would recommend following your dreams to everyone out there.

Drs. Nikolien Martina-Doorenbos Bio

Nikolien is the founder and director of Moms & More in The Netherlands. She makes ambitious moms happy again with themselves and their lives. So women can do that what makes them most happy and at the same time experience harmony in work and life.

Nikolien is mom of daughter Emilia and son Alessio. She knows how life is an ambitious mom juggling with all balls (and occasionally drop one). She is allergic to complainants, victims and empty glasses. She loves chocolate, wine and chicklits. Nikolien is the very first Creatrix® Facilitator and Woman's Transformologist® in Europe, certified the Australian Institute of Women International.

Furthermore, she is a certified NLP Master Practitioner, certified DISC trainer, and completed several courses aimed at women's health, personal and intuitive development. She is a respected speaker and author of the book *"Juggling Kids and a Career, A Practical Guide for Working Mothers"*.

Moms and More

Drs. Nikolien Martina-Doorenbos – Netherlands

In this day and age, we as women often forget to trust our gut feeling, our instinct, our intuition. We take decisions based on our ratio, our thoughts. We decide only after we carefully considered all pro's and con's, and frequently are rejecting the wisdom of our inner voice.

I was one of those women. Having an academic background, over the years I de-learned to listen to my heart and followed my head instead. Until Emilia, my first-born, joined our lives. I noticed that when I was pregnant all the attention and care went to me, the mom-to-be.

However, after birth all eyes were on the baby. And me? I did not know how to manage this big change in life, missed (professional) support and unbiased acknowledgement. I felt lonely, guilty and disappointed, lacking fulfilment and purpose in my life. (Later I learned that I was not the only one, and that 90% of the new moms are overwhelmed and find it hard to adjust). And whether it was due to the hormonal rollercoaster or the fact that I was confronted with leaving a legacy and the fragility of life, I felt the urge to start coaching other moms. Even though I was a full-time headhunter at one of the most prestige executive search firms in the world and just had a baby. However, that drive was so strong and intense that I could not neglect it. And even though I was coaching in the evenings and in the weekends next to my regular working hours as headhunter, I just had to do this.

Fast forward to end 2015… My coaching business had grown and I developed into a recognised full-time coach for moms. However, I was not satisfied with the results I got. Yes I gave women insight and helped them change, but I felt that insights were just not good enough, that the change was not long lasting enough. I missed a superior coaching method for females, breaking women through fast, painless, and for good. As I didn't want to leave my kids behind in order to be a regular coach, I wanted to be an extraordinary one. A coach where people would say: Nikolien you've changed my life!

And I was wondering: how come that with all those coaches and therapists around, and with all those self-help books, methods, programmes and challenges available, still women become stuck and stay stuck? That meant perhaps that the methods used were not good enough? That it was not us failing the method, but that the method failed us?

I made a wish list of all the things I needed and wanted in a modality in order to be an outstanding coach, just for my own reflection I thought. But several days later I suddenly felt a strong urge, a deep inner push to post this list online in a group of female entrepreneurs. With the question if someone knew something that would match with this list. And you must know that this group has thousands of members. I got one reply on my question from a woman all the way on the other side of the world, in Australia (and mind you due to time differences, it was really a "coincidence": one hour earlier or later, and she hadn't seen the post).

This woman directed me to the Institute of Women International and the Creatrix® method. I did my research, and Oh my, it ticked all boxes! I went on a Skype call with Maz Schirmer, owner of Institute of Women International, and within one (1!) hour I decided to travel all the way to Australia and follow the Creatrix® Facilitator and Woman's Transformologist® training. If you would look at this from a rational viewpoint I would be crazy: leaving a baby and a small child behind for over 3 weeks, travel to the other side of the world for a method and a company I did not have any experience with at all, nor did anyone in Europe has. Investing heavily in the unknown.

However I trusted my instinct, my intuition, my gut feeling. I followed my heart. And that has thrown me into the most amazing journey of my life: I became the first Creatrix® Facilitator and Woman's Transformologist® in Europe and are about to become the first Institute of Women International trainer too. I get to meet so many inspiring women all across the globe, and can be of true and meaningful value by not only changing, but truly saving women's lives. And most importantly: I learned to really trust female intuition and by just following your heart – even though it goes against all odds will give you miracles!

"A woman is the full circle. Within her is the power to create, nurture and transform."
Diane Mariechild

> **Jenny Strong Bio**
>
> Jenny Strong brings energy and expertise to the table to help clients reach their goals as an Associate Director for Macquarie Bank.
>
> When Jenny isn't helping business owners and high net worth investors grow their wealth, she spends quality time with her supportive husband and her beautiful daughter Thalia.

Thinking Happy

Jenny Strong – Australia

They say 'change is as good as a holiday'. I believe this to be absolutely true although it is not without its challenges. However, I firmly believe a strong positive mindset, a 'can do' attitude and a great support network allows you to overcome most obstacles. My name is Jenny Strong and I would like to share my story.

It would be fair to say I grew up in a less than conventional household deep in the suburbs of Brisbane. 5 sisters including 2 sets of twins and a mere 5 year gap between eldest and youngest raised by a single (very hardworking and patient parent!!!). Our household was underpinned by trust (rather than rules- because let's face it what parent can keep track of 6 active kids!), a focus on independence and a belief that anything and everything was possible if you worked hard enough.

Our household was certainly not the richest in dollars however we were extraordinarily rich in our love and support of each other. We were raised to believe that the world was filled with amazing opportunities and that life was to be 'lived' with a sense of adventure and enthusiasm.

In my early 30s I met an amazing Canadian man who would change my life forever and we were married in 2013. Then in 2014 and 2015 our life dramatically changed. This started with some serious health concerns which I am happy to report, we successfully overcame. Shortly thereafter our beautiful daughter Thalia was born and we became parents for the first time. Whilst adapting to a dramatic lifestyle change (as any mum knows- the joys of round the clock feeding and nappies, feeding and nappies, feeding and nappies……..), my husband was offered and accepted a position in NSW. This role involved significant travel and time away from home.

Within 2 weeks we had given up all that we knew, all our families and friends for life in the big smoke. In the background my career had progressed well. I had enjoyed 16 great years of employment with Macquarie Bank and had been promoted a number of times to Associate Director. My work is not just a 'job' for me, it is a career. It is something I do for myself, fills me with pride and it is an important part of my life. With my husbands relocation, Macquarie Bank kindly agreed to relocate me to our Sydney (head) office.

In February 2016 I returned to work on a full time basis. This represented a steep learning curve and many new challenges for me in the sales arena and client management. The geographic landscape was foreign – I had no contacts, no profile and a 1 year old who remains top priority. In addition we faced the inevitable long bouts of illness as our baby entered daycare for the first time. Most mums would know what I am talking about!! It honestly felt like my little one and I were sick every other week.

The game changers for me have been a supportive employer who has given me wonderful support and true flexibility in my work environment. In addition, I have a strong personal philosophy that the difference between a good day and a bad day is my state of mind and that starts and stops with me. Positivity, energy and enthusiasm feels good and is infectious! It is great for me, great for the workplace and no coincidence has impacted my performance in a great way.

I am a true believer in the power of 'thinking happy', coupled with great personal organisation and planning (we have the chalk boards and multiple schedules at home to prove it- plan to succeed as they say). I tell myself every morning that anything is possible and to keep on 'dreaming, believing, creating and achieving'. It has been a challenging year however the most rewarding of my life and one that I will look back on fondly in years to come.

Dedicated to all the hard working mums out there.

> **Karen Darke Bio**
>
> Karen Darke is a British Paralympic cyclist, Paratriathlete, adventurer, author and motivational speaker. She is a full-time athlete with the British Para-Cycling Team and squeezes adventures in where possible between training and other work.

Life is an Adventure

Karen Darke – UK

Becoming paralysed in a rock-climbing accident at age 21 left me facing a choice. I, as an active soul and a lover of the outdoors, I could sit around and feel miserable about my new situation, or I could face up to it. I could try and make the most of my new circumstances, and focus on what I could do instead of what I couldn't.

Since then, I have pursued alternative ways to access the outdoors – canoeing, sit-skiing and hand-cycling. I have been lucky to hand-cycle in various corners of the world, including Central Asia and the Himalaya, the Karakoram and the length of the Japanese archipelago, New Zealand, parts of Europe and shortly, the length of Chile's Patagonian wilderness. Thanks to many good friends and acquaintances, life has become one giant adventure; from sea kayaking along the coastlines of British Columbia and Alaska, skiing across the Greenland icecap, climbing the kilometre-high vertical rock-face of El Capitan, and kayaking through the fjords of Patagonia. I have adopted the philosophy that to learn the most from life we should challenge our constraints, adopt a positive mindset and support each other to be the best we can be.

The night before I was paralysed, I commented to a friend "I would rather be dead than paralysed. I can't imagine anything worse". How wrong could I have been? We are all stronger than we might think, braver than we might believe, more able than we might feel. It is only when life forces us to have to find those inner resources that they have the chance to appear.

More recently, life has led me to a Paralympic journey with the British Cycling Team, a silver medal in the London Paralympics 2012 and a gold in Rio 2016. I fit other wilderness adventures in when I can – the healing power of nature is something that feels important to me, especially to rebalance after hard or stressful times in life.

What is life if it isn't an adventure? I'm constantly amazed by what can be achieved if we set our heart and mind to it. It's all about finding belief, confidence, motivation and commitment. And of course, friends. Then there are perhaps no limits.

Christine Rudolph Bio

Christine Rudolph is currently ranked in the top 2% of Ray White Agents internationally, having being awarded a prestigious Alan While Elite Performer awards in both 2016 and 2015.

Christine has also been awarded the Ray White Award for Excellence in Marketing 2015 and is consistently ranked in the top 5 Courier Mail agents for Queensland.

- 2016 Alan White Elite Performer Award
- 2015 Alan White Elite Performer Award
- 2015 Ray White Queensland Excellence in Marketing Award
- 2016 Top 5 Courier Mail Advertiser
- 2016 100% Ray White Customer Service Satisfaction

Discover Your Why

Christine Rudolph – Australia

One of my favourite sayings about success is fall down seven times, get up eight.

25 years ago as a starry eyed television presenter, marrying my handsome prince charming and believing in the blissfully happy ever after fairytale, I had no idea that the significant setbacks which lay ahead, would one day be the foundation for my career in Real Estate.

My husband and I worked very hard in our early 20's, saved enough to buy property, renovated and built up a small portfolio at a young age. He had a flourishing business and together we had big dreams for our future.

We were blessed with the birth of a beautiful daughter and being the eldest of 8 children, I regarded motherhood as a woman's ultimate gift and responsibility. I swapped my career as a successful journalist and newsreader, to embrace motherhood and support my husband in his business.

Misfortunate unexpectedly struck in our blissful early years of marriage and our world quickly unravelled. My husband was no longer able to work, our business was sold and I went back to work to support us in an attempt to save us from going bankrupt.

We had no choice but to sell everything, the pressure cost us our marriage and I was left to bring up our daughter alone, educating her and keeping a roof over our heads.

The experience of losing everything and selling our properties, gave me a less than positive insight into the real estate industry and a strong dislike for agents.

We naively made every wrong mistake…choosing agents who over quoted and lost hundreds of thousands of dollars in the process. I made a quiet commitment to myself to one day go into real estate to be of service to others and to provide not only transparency, but more importantly, the support and empathy required by clients in such stressful situations.

10 years ago, while working in a secure, well paid corporate position and seeing 40 nearing the horizon, the sudden death of my beautiful father in 2006 was a turning point which made me realise life was short and there was no time for regrets. I decided to take the leap of faith and follow my calling to be in real estate.

As a single mother, with a mortgage to pay and young daughter in a private school, this was not a decision I took lightly and was fortunate to find a wonderful employer, Christina Guidotti, now an international speaker and mentor, who gave me my break.

The lessons I have learned from my failures have been key to my business success.

1. No matter how many setbacks in life, success is in remaining resilient and persistent.
2. Having personally walked in the shoes of many of my clients, experiencing death, divorce, debt, downsizing has given me an

incredible insight and capacity to provide support and empathy when selling their homes.

3. The level of service we provide and the amount of effort put into real estate are rewarded not only financially, but more importantly, with the respect and gratitude of our clients.
4. Treat our clients the way we would like to be treated. I always think back to my worst experiences with agents and remind myself constantly of the significant responsibility we have in helping our client's achieve the best possible price for their biggest asset and moving them with the greatest care and respect to the next chapter of their lives.
5. Our greatest setbacks in life are often our greatest gifts.
6. It's never too late to start again. What the mind can conceive, it truly can achieve.

Remaining on the real estate rollercoaster has always been about focusing on a long term view. Having seen a GFC and challenging markets, success is about riding out the difficult times, looking for solutions, surrounding yourself with mentors, people who believe in you and most importantly, backing yourself to believe that you will succeed.

Many say real estate is a competitive environment. In my own case, I have never focussed on the competition, but instead, focussed solely on continuing to strive to be a better agent and provide the highest level of service and committment to my clients. I believe in taking a long term view and building a business based on solid relationships and integrity.

Finally, the most important motivator for me always at the forefront of my mind, is;- What is my Why?

At times when I felt like giving up, I've only had to look at the beautiful little face of my daughter who depended on me and think about giving her a good life and being a strong role model. I am so proud that she too has chosen real estate as her career, working in Sydney's Eastern Suburbs.

My why continues to be to leave a legacy not only to my daughter, my nieces and nephews and siblings, but to others of all ages in this industry. Above all, I want to be respected as an agent who is authentic and with integrity.

I am an empty nester now and look forward to the tremendous rewards real estate offers in having choices. For me these are the flexibility to travel to visit my daughter and my extended family as well as the ability to create a wonderful financial freedom for the future. I have been fortunate it has provided me the means to slowly rebuild a small property portfolio and my next big dream is to help my daughter into her own home.

And finally being ever the romantic, I look forward to enjoying the ultimate rewards of this incredible career with the financial security to revel in the golden years of my life, flying first class off into the sunset with my future prince charming!

Cassandra Austin Bio

Cassandra joined the food service industry as a 15 year old, Women in the commercial kitchen were an anomaly 25 years later, she is an accomplished Chef, Consultant, Recipe developer, and Culinary Judge. With qualifications as a Commercial chef, Restaurateur and Teacher, she has now branched into Diet, Nutrition and Food Psychology, her niche in the market is supporting people, mostly Women who want more from a healthy diet, eating, physical and mental concerns in a personalised and private forum.

Success came at a cost to her mental and physical health and after years of ignoring it. Through food and a healthy lifestyle, she has found many ways to reverse the damage and have a wealth of skills to help you cook yourself to better health.

She has committed to improving people's life styles, networking and career opportunities for females struggling with health and general wellness "To be the best that you can be".

"Cass is living proof that you don't have to be one of the boys in attire and attitude to succeed in the culinary world. Whatever she sets out to do, she gets done."

Be The Best You Can Be

Cassandra Austin – Australia

After leaving school at age 15 years, I began an apprenticeship as a chef. This was significant because, at that time, I was the only girl in my class at the technical college course and it was rare to have a woman working in a restaurant kitchen. In fact, during a work experience period, with a chef, he explained to me that he didn't employ women to work in his kitchen. However, I had a passion for working with "food" so I persevered and waited, until he gave me my chance.

Despite these common beliefs, I worked my way through all the negativity and became dogmatic, through work, to achieve my goals. In time, my "dreams" were realised and I had my own restaurant and I became successful and respected in the hospitality industry.

Even though I had proven to the world that a woman could be a respected, and successful, restaurateur I started to notice that, firstly my body was reacting to the extremely, long hours of work. As well, I became, psychologically, exhausted because of the cumulative anxiety that I experienced worrying about maintaining my success. In retrospect, it was clear that I had no balance in my life but only obsessed with working harder.

Consequently, I required medical intervention meaning prescribed medication, and counselling, to combat the anxiety/depression as well as the inability to control my weight. After some six months, I felt worse because I lost the energy I needed which meant a reliance on medications I had to maintain the work and, hence, the continuing success of my business. After some time, I began to reflect on my life, work and general health when I had an epiphany that would change me forever.

Successful people in life achieve their goals through hard work or by working smarter. I began to analyse myself and realised that I had proven myself, worked ridiculous hours but at the cost of my health. Proving myself to the world may have been achieved had I not "pushed" my body to exhaustion and ill health but, simply, may have taken a longer time. It was at this time in my life that I made the decision to change, be more proactive, and take more care of my physical, and psychological self religiously, I would eat a varied, healthy diet and began exercising by walking regularly, rejecting cigarettes in favour of attending to the needs of my body and my mind.

From then I noticed that weekly changes in my life such as that I became fitter, stronger and calmer, more controlled, in my mind. Also I felt happier as I completely, changed my life but still managed the restaurant, taught commercial cookery at college level and judging culinary competitions. I recall people telling me I looked 10 years younger and I felt it.

As well as continuing my increasing responsibilities, I began doing charity work with the Australian Culinary Federation which I enjoyed and felt fulfilled, then I met my husband "also a chef" who purchased my restaurant so we could spend more time together. In recent times I have finished 8 years as part of the World Association of Chef's Societies', doing charity work as a committee member and regional representative of the Women's Leadership forum.

As well I have been involved in contract consulting, recipes development, testing and costing together with the production of cook books and videos for my professional Industry, working and travelling the world with work and my husband.

Throughout my journey with food and a healthy lifestyle, I believe I have found strategies in developing better health and to reverse the deleterious effects of poor diet. By studying diet and nutrition, food psychology and wellness coaching, I have developed programs online or personalised, that include some 10 workshops to empower women to learn practical, effective and evidence based skills to enhance your lifestyle.

My commitment, and focus, has been to improve people's lives by adopting the motto "Be the best you can be".

"Stop wearing your wishbone where your backbone ought to be."
Elizabeth Gilbert

Kate Maree O'Brien Bio

After coming through tremendous challenges, Kate became a recognized national leader in her field as a registered nurse, speaking at international health conferences, being nominated for a special regional health award for her national work in training doctors & nurses throughout New Zealand as powerful change agents & was a finalist for the New Zealand Emerging Speaker of the Year in 2013.

She received high accolades for her work as a national project manager with her work being featured at national conferences.

Game Changer

Kate Maree O'Brien – New Zealand

"A personality is heavy to carry when you're not standing in the truth of your soul."

Kate O'Brien is a visionary, and global voice for bold leadership, playing it big & living from truth. She is a powerful stand for what's possible for humanity. Kate holds a strong space which calls people to move beyond their conditioned reality & patterns of smallness, stuckness & limitation; to deeply own their truth & expand into their fullest potential.

After coming through tremendous challenges (including drug addiction, anorexia & depression), Kate became a recognized national leader in her field as a registered nurse, speaking at international health conferences, being nominated for a special regional health award for her national work in training doctors & nurses throughout New Zealand as powerful change agents & was a finalist for the New Zealand Emerging Speaker of the Year in 2013. She received high accolades for her work as a national project manager with her work being featured at national conferences.

Despite a thriving career, Kate let it all go to pursue her life calling of empowering billions globally to wake up and deeply own their power.

Alongside her husband Henare, she co-founded the GameChanger Global Summit, an annual event connecting the top thought leaders of our generation. On her stage, she attracts luminary greats such as Jack Canfield, John Gray, Brendon Burchard, Marci Shimoff, Dr John Demartini, T Harv Eker, Gregg Braden, Brandon Bays, Sonia Choquette, Eben Pagan and many, many more.

Sharon Jurd Bio

Sharon Jurd is a fast business growth specialist, and an international author and speaker. Looking after business owners through a number of formats including one on one coaching, seminars, consulting, staff training and group brainstorming.

More Time, More Freedom and More Money

Sharon Jurd – Australia

At 29, I believed I was doing just fine like everyone else. I was happily married and I was blessed with 2 amazing kids. But life, as we know it, is full of surprises and mine came quite unexpectedly.

On June 30, 2000 I woke up with a massive headache. I shrugged it off and downed a painkiller to kill the pain. I didn't think about it much since I had been experiencing headaches on and off for a while and taking painkillers always made me feel better. It was a typical day just like all the other days before it but I was wrong.

My husband who worked as an interstate truck driver at that time was at home so I asked him to look after the kids while I did some grocery shopping. While at the grocery store my head started to throb again and my vision blurred. It got so bad that I had to stop what I was doing and I drove back home.

While driving I had to stop the car twice and waited patiently for my vision to clear before I resumed driving. Even though it kind of bothered me I thought nothing of it like I always do since migraines randomly happen to busy people like me. I arrived home safely and went to bed with a wet washer on my forehead.

Later on, I visited my parent's house but as soon as I got inside I felt I needed to lie down. After a couple of minutes I got up to tell my father I was feeling ill, when all of a sudden I collapsed on the floor. On that day, I suffered my very first stroke.

You see, I am the type of person who liked being in control and I think my security stems from me being able to control the things around me from my home to my business. When I suffered a stroke my life crumbled before my eyes. Communication was difficult and so was mobility. This meant I had to rely on others around me.

It was during these times when I realized that no one in my family actually knew my normal routine, not even my husband. Although they had vague ideas about what I did they didn't really know the full details. I had structured my life around me and I was responsible for its success both in my life and in my business.

Little did I realise if I'm not there everything else would fail because not a single soul knew how I ran things. And what made it all the more difficult was the fact that I had to run a business while at the same time look after our kids. My stroke was definitely something I failed to prepare for.

As my strength and speech improved during recovery I started incorporating strategies in both my personal life and my business. Through the use of simple systems I was able to successfully gain control despite my physical absence. My goal was for my family and my business to grow and thrive during trying times.

The reason I am sharing my story is to show people that despite what you may go through, if you persevere and not give up on your dreams, everything will fall into place. I designed my business so that it can stand the test of time even without me being there and now I teach people all over the world how to do just that. Every business is vulnerable at some stage and I am living testimony proving that if you do it right (incorporating effective strategies) your business will surely grow fast so you can have more time to do the things you've always wanted to do. My vision for every entrepreneur is to have more time, more money and more life.

Lisa Druxman Bio

Nationally recognized as an expert in the field of fitness, particularly pre and postnatal, mompreneur Lisa Druxman is the creator of FIT4MOM®. Her programs such as Stroller Strides, Fit4Baby and Body Back are all part of the Fit4Mom family.

The FIT4MOM franchise has consistently been ranked by numerous publications as one of the fastest growing franchises in the country. Lisa has created one of the top companies for moms to work for according to Working Mother magazine.

Lisa Druxman is a mom on a mission! It is her hope to inspire all moms to live a healthier life.

Mom On A Mission

Lisa Druxman - USA

You know when you hear about those lightbulb moments? That's what I had. I was on a stroller walk with my new baby and I was filled with the following thoughts...

"This is the best hour of my day. All moms should workout with their stroller."

"I don't know any mom who is happy with her body. I bet I could help them"

"I have so many questions about motherhood. Where am I going to get the answers?"

"I so don't want to leave Jacob to go back to work."

And then the lightbulb lit.

I could start a stroller fitness workout. I can help moms get back in shape and they can help me with everything I need to know about being a mom. I even named it on that walk. Stroller Strides.

And that's what I did. I started a stroller strides workout in my neighborhood. I just had a handful of moms but it quickly became my village. Apparently I wasn't the only one looking for a village because the concept took off. I hired local fitness instructors to teach more classes in San Diego. I didn't have to go back to my old work after all.

By the end of the first year, we had 1,000 moms taking Stroller Strides classes. Within just a few months, we started getting calls from around the country; women were looking to join or start Stroller Strides. I didn't know how I was going to do it but knew that I wanted all moms to get the support and strength we got from these classes. And I loved the idea of giving other women the career opportunity that I had in running Stroller Strides.

So we decided to franchise the business. We now have nearly 2,000 class locations nationwide. And as my kids grew (now 15 and 11), so did the business. We added FIT4BABY, Stroller Barre, Body Back and even a run club for moms. We are now celebrating 15 years in business.

It has been an incredible journey and story along the way. But there is no overnight success. We have fallen down many a time and the lessons learned have often been hard ones. But when you have a passion and a purpose for what you do, you find a way around, over or under any obstacle that comes your way.

We are big fans of Simon Sinek's Start With Why. Our why is to give women the strength for motherhood. This isn't just about sets and reps. This is about helping moms get out of overwhelm and into a life that they love. All of our programs help moms achieve health and happiness at every stage of motherhood.

Know what I've learned over the last 15 years? That leadership in business is the same as leadership in family.

1. Be true to your values
2. Have a mission
3. Be focused on what's important
4. Take full responsibility
5. Always be learning

Narelle Shiell Bio

A qualified counsellor specialising in using the transactional analysis model for growth and change, Narelle is also a trainer, speaker and coach (life & work) and loves co-creating outcomes that inspire women to lead in their lives.

You will find Narelle approaches her clients with good humor and a lightness that provides a gentle and safe place to explore the depths of your whole being.

Narelle has a corporate background in administration and finance management working for employers such as Logi-Tech, Flinders University and the South Australian Film Corporation; and in Media Sales working for Fairfax Media and other smaller rural publications. In her own business Narelle offers a range of coaching, counselling and training services to individuals, community groups and corporate clients.

Narelle holds a number of professional qualifications including Polarity Therapy, Remedial Massage and Training & Assessment. She has also undertaken a number of non accredited courses to further her own personal and professional development.

Honour Your Journey, Create Your Life

Narelle Shiell – Australia

I have not always been a professional coach and counsellor but I have always been the accidental one. For many years I worked in the corporate arena firstly in administration and finance management and then I moved onto advertising and media sales. I have had the pleasure of more than one career in this life and in all of them I found the common thread I loved the most was coaching, counselling and training – these skills came naturally to me.

Alongside all of this great career stuff my personal life for many years was a trainwreck. There is not a high enough word limit in this article for all the 'stuff' so i will share the highlights that have helped shaped me.

- Major car accident at 18 and my parents and immediately moved overseas – all in a 3 month window. This led to a major health crises where I discovered the power of natural therapies. I later trained in Remedial Massage, Polarity Therapy, Counselling and Training as a direct result of this experience.
- Married in my early 20s and 2 beautiful babies by 28, divorced at 30. I learned more about myself in this time that I have ever known and after divorce I came to know my own strength. I also learnt a lot about people too.
- Further health crises in my early 30s and ultimately diagnosed with multiple autoimmune diseases. From this I learned about my capacity for self love and regulating how and where I was spending my time and energy.
- Workplace bullying in 2010 that resulted in a trip to the ER with panic so severe it was first thought a cardiac issue. Here I subsequently decided that I would never work for anyone else ever again because I was bullied for my ability and not lack of it.
- Re-married at 41 and moved from Adelaide to Townsville. I learned that life always comes full circle and that nothing 'bad' or 'hard' is forever. I learned how to truly love someone else and still love and honour myself.

Most 'healers' become that way because they have their own wounds to first 'heal'. I am no exception. So why am I telling you this?

I firmly believe you cannot truly love and embrace who you are and at the same time hate the experiences and decisions that got you there. You are after all a sum total of every moment of your life until right now.

The path to true self love for me was fraught with many things that in order to heal I had to learn to love, see the silver lining in and find a way to view in a positive light.

It is hard to see things like bullying, which I had also experienced in high school, positively; nor is it easy to understand why your body may be struck down with dis-ease when you actively go out of your way to nurture it and treat it well. And like many faced with these types of challenges I spent a lot of time asking 'why me'?

The answer? Well there are many – it has given me insight I would have otherwise never had, compassion I would have never felt and the ability to see deeply into people and situations to find the gold among the pain, hurt and challenges life might be throwing up.

In recent years I have created my life around the 'challenges' I live with rather than by fighting them. These serve as a beautiful reminder to slow down when I try to run too fast. My natural tendency is be busy and live fast and being slowed down actually helps me see the beauty in life, each moment and 'stop to smell the roses' I have settled into a beautiful slice of North Queensland paradise and run my practice from home and in the online space enabling me to work with clients and collaborate with peers from anywhere in the world. I especially love working with women who know they want to make a change to how they live their lives whether at home, work or in their business. Women who want to step up their game and experience life in a new and more positive, meaningful way.

"Do not compare yourself to others. Stay focused on your own journey and leave footprints behind."
Anon

Tracey Mathers Bio

Tracey Mathers is a trusted advisor to those wanting to build and maintain success in business. With retail running through her veins, third generation retailer Tracey Mathers has been continuing the family tradition for over 24 years.

As the Granddaughter of the founder of Mathers Shoes it was inevitable she would become a leading retailer in her field. Having had up to six stores she has learnt to deal with all areas of running a successful business.

Stay True To Yourself

Tracey Mathers – Australia

As a third generation shoe retailer from the Mathers shoe family, I always felt like one of the lucky ones. I remember sitting on my Dad's lap in his office in Mary Street, Brisbane City, at about the age of 6 and saying one day this will be all mine. I will run this business one day. That was not meant to be, but I am grateful for the journey it started me on, and the incredible values it instilled in me.

I started working casually for Mathers Shoes when I was 14, and I truly loved it and knew that when I finished school I wanted a full time career in the business. I was so excited about this because I already knew I wanted to travel the world, buying amazing shoes for women that would make them feel fabulous, empowered and beautiful.

At 17, I asked for a meeting with my dad. You did this in my household when you had something serious to discuss and I told him I had decided to join the family company. He was very excited. However I said to him, if this is to work you need to stay out of my career going forward. I need to do this on my own, I need the proof that I am worthy of climbing the ladder not because of my last name but on my talent and merit. He agreed to that, and so my journey began.

It was difficult at first. Being the boss's daughter taught me very quickly how to manage conflict, how to work out who is with you, and who isn't, and most importantly, how to handle the ones who aren't. All this at the age of 17 made me grow up extremely quickly.

I survived, I loved it, but eventually the day came when my father organised a successful buy-out by Woolworth America, and I was shattered. My dream of potentially taking over and being that third generation to run the company was now gone. That did not last long thankfully, as the new owners were fabulous, very motivational and I loved working for them. I moved further up the ladder and was learning heaps.

One day, they decided to close a division of the company which was a more upmarket branding. In my opinion, this was going to leave a huge gap in the marketplace. I had recently found a fabulous new retail site in Brisbane City and decided it was time to do my own thing. So with a fire in my belly and a business plan in my hand, I jumped on a plane to Italy and went shoe shopping. That was the start of Tracey Mathers Shoe Studio in 1991.

I owned my retail stores for 25 years. I had massive highs and some impressive lows but what a journey it has been and what I have learned, both good and bad, along the way has set me up for my new career path.

I decided to sell my stores. After 25 years, I just felt it was the right time to put all I have learnt over the years into helping others. I am now mentoring, speaking and consulting to small and medium businesses who can benefit in any area in which I have expertise. I am absolutely loving my new career. I now help others to achieve their goals, to help them get positioned where they need to be, for the results they are going after. And I am there with them on the journey the whole way.

Being in small business can be a really hard, often we feel alone, and we have so many huge decisions to make, often they have to be made on our own.

A few big lessons I have learnt along the way are:

1. It is okay if others don't believe in you, if they don't get your "why" as long as you do. Don't ever let anyone take away your dreams or your goals, stay true to your beliefs and stay true to yourself always.

2. Surround yourself with people that are smarter than you. People that are going to challenge you, teach you, support you and believe in you. This is when magic happens, and we get great results on our own journey.

3. Don't ever give up, we are only limited by our own imagination.

"Behind every successful women is a tribe of other successful women who have her back."
Anon

Grace Alviar Viray Bio

Grace Alviar Viray is currently a freelance social media strategist and contact creator for several international companies and websites. She just recently launched her personal blog online which is one of her personal goals.

When she's not in front of her laptop, Grace loves spending time with her amazing husband Troy and their adorable daughter Kahlila in their lovely home in Davao City, Philippines.

Juggling a Virtual Career while Being a Full Time Wife and Mom

Grace Alviar Viray – Philippines

I believe that when you finally know your priorities, God instructs the universe to open up opportunities so you can have what you need and want at the same time. I am Grace Alviar Viray and this is my story.

I grew up in a small town in Los Banos, Laguna, Philippines and was born to a father who was an engineer and a mother who was a public school teacher. Growing up, I have gone through a lot of challenges: from selling our own house to moving from one small apartment to another, to losing both my parents.

At 14, I lost my father to a blood disease, and at 18 my mother was diagnosed with cancer. It was never easy but I was always positive. Fortunately, after chemo and radiation treatments, my mother recovered, and I was able to go back to school and earned a university degree while I was working part-time jobs.

Life worked well for me after I earned my diploma, I was able to get my licence as a Registered Nutritionist-Dietitian in the Philippines and I even got a job as Nutrition Representative in the biggest food company in the country. At the age of 25, I lived my dream job in the corporate world until my mother was again diagnosed with another form of cancer. She passed away that year and I was more than devastated.

I resigned from that job and went hopping from one role to another. I became a college instructor, a nutrition resource speaker, even a sales coordinator. I felt that I didn't have any responsibilities and I only needed to take care of myself and never minded what role I had until I landed a role I really loved: corporate training. For some reason, I had to leave that job again. It was like I had to start all over again.

Eventually, when I had my own family, things started to fall into place. I started my virtual career as a Business English trainer, until I was given opportunities to write for several news and media websites. I also became part of REJS and Inspiring Women Today by Nikki Taylor where I learned a lot about marketing and global communication. Currently, I am a freelance social media strategist and content curator for several international companies and websites. I also launched my personal blog online named www.whatevergracemeans.com in April 2017 where I get to share my musings and also feature other bloggers globally.

I may not be working in a corporate office building like I used to, but now I earn even more than what I used to earn while I get to work with amazing people globally! And the best part about my virtual career is that I get to be with my husband and daughter almost 24/7, something that my previous roles can never offer.

Today, I'm not as restless as I was before: I believe that I already have learned my priorities and God is leading me where I should go, one step at a time.

Every woman has her own inspiring story to tell, and I believe this is mine. I still have many dreams I'd love to fulfill soon, and I'd like to inspire and help other mothers like me who would also like to have a virtual career while taking care of their children.

Know your priorities: this is what will lead you where you really to want to be!

Hershey Hilado Bio

Named as one of the Most Influential Millennial Entrepreneur that exists today. At 24 years of age she has built three international businesses; 8TASKS a high level offshore outsourcing company based in the Philippines, creativevortex.com.au a creative and branding agency & ohmagosh.com a women's fashion eCommerce business she founded 4 years ago and recently nominated as one of the Top 50 Most Innovative and Exciting eCommerce Stores in Australia for 2016.

She was also named as one of the Top 80 Women2Watch in 2017 by Remodista stealing the 3rd spot in Australia among 10 Australians and 70 other women from different parts of the world.

Today, she is on a mission to help other Entrepreneurs, Business Owners and Startups launch and scale their businesses forward.

Serve, Surrender, Impact

Hershey Hilado – Australia

Hershey Hilado is not your typical 24 year old. Her difficult upbringing enabled her to develop the resilience and ability to influence others by example. Recently nominated as one of the 30 under 30 Influencive Entrepreneurs 2016, she is unstoppable with a purpose to SERVE, SURRENDER and IMPACT millions of lives.

Growing up in an environment of physical and emotional abuse she became a parent to 7 of her siblings at a mere age of 14. Her father was murdered by her own uncle when she was 12. She got into shoplifting when she was 13 to survive. Her own Mother forced her to marry a man 3 times her age when she was 16 for money.

After escaping that terrible ordeal she became homeless for 2 years until she found her relatives on the Father's side who took her in until she found her way to Australia when she was 18.

She worked in McDonalds as a crew member and as a Security Control Room Operator for a few years until she realized that her calling was far greater than just being good at her job. Her purpose was far greater than simply earning and surviving. After reading Robert Kiyosaki's Rich Dad Poor Dad book she then quit her job few months later and started her first business back in November 2013.

Today, she runs 2 businesses, a Women's Fashion Label called Ohmagosh sold in over 15 countries across the globe and Creative Vortex where Entrepreneurs, Startups and Business Owners can purchase pre-made branding packages.

Her passion and purpose stretches beyond overcoming adversity, running a business and Entrepreneurship. As a Philanthropist she is one of the Ambassadors for The Freedom Hub, a non for profit organization that helps rebuild the lives of survivors of Human Trafficking and Sex Slavery in Australia.

She speaks for those who needed a voice. She is a hustler, global speaker and passionate human being that truly lives her life with so much gratitude.

She is one of the most Inspirational and Influential Female Entrepreneur of this generation and now on a mission to inspire and impact others through her journey and stories of the world's most powerful and successful Millennial Entrepreneurs.

Dina Del Rosario Josue Bio

Dina Josue is a Certified Chef and a Registered Nutritionist-Dietitian. She always has the eye for details. She has an exceptional background in food management and service. A graduate of BS Nutrition in the University of the Philippines with professional license in Nutrition-Dietetics, Chef Dina is well versed when it comes to food research and development and culinary arts.

She had training alongside with Chef MC at the Broadmoor, Colorado Springs, USA and worked with international chefs at Atlantis the Palm, Dubai.

Chef Dina also chases after her 15-month old son, Matthew Dylan and takes care of her husband Chef Michael when she isn't preparing amazing food and calculating diets. An advocate of healthy eating and breastfeeding, Chef Dina always makes sure she walks her talk!

On Fire for Healthy Eating: From Passion to Mission

Dina Del Rosario Josue – Philippines

As a girl whose name was taken from the scientific name of a fire tree "delonix regia," I know I am unique; of course, who would else be named after a fire tree? I am the only known Chef Dietitian in our city, Puerto Princesa, in the Philippines.

Actually, there's really not a "worst moment" in my life story. My parents brought me up to be God-fearing, carefree and I am loved by everybody since I am the youngest. Loved by everybody may mean I am more dependent on my parents than any of my siblings. I can say that I had trouble deciding on my own. That is why in college, my mom suggested or should I say decided for me to take up BS Nutrition. I have always wanted to be a chef but growing up in a family of academically inclined individuals.

I guess I should finish a university degree first before pursuing my passion. There was no regrets, really. I believed that for one to grow maturely, he has to decide on his own. Four and a half years in college plus a licensure exam in dietetics is not a walk in the park. I remember those days when I just wanted to quit school and be a cook. That's what I really wanted to do in the first place. Good thing I followed mom's advice. That road I took was actually a good investment in my career. Being the only chef dietitian in my town was an advantage. I am only seeing now the product of my hard work throughout the years.

Flashback in 2009, I made my own decision to study culinary arts. That was the most exciting year because finally, I can live my passion. My family behind me to support is really important and encouraging. However, to graduate from a culinary school doesn't make you a chef. You have to take the lowest role in the kitchen brigade when you start working in a real kitchen setting. I had an opportunity to train in the US and work in Dubai. Those times when reality strikes, I was having a hard time because I felt like I didn't belong. I remember asking myself, "What am I doing? I am here hiding in pots and pans when I know I can do more to life!" I really thought I was going to be stuck. Doing a 12-hr shift everyday even took a toll on my health. I was diagnosed with PCOS (Polycystic Ovarian Syndrome) and I felt devastated.

This kind of lifestyle is slowly killing me! I should really start being healthy! Then I realized, every decision you make in life molds you into better version of you. I decided to pick myself up and use what I learned about health and proper nutrition & culinary arts. One secret to what I have right now is staying focused on my goals and strive to be better but also grounded everyday; then, everything follows.

In 2014, my husband, Chef Michael Custodio, invited me to go home to the Philippines from Dubai and suggested to start a Thai Food Restaurant "Inthai". It was an old brand which I started back in culinary days but then halted for a while because of my training in the US. It was actually a re-branding. Inthai is a modern Thai food restaurant here in Palawan, Philippines. It was featured in local TV as a healthy food restaurant. Having the right staff, kitchen and experience, we decided to put up a healthy food delivery as well in which personalized and calculated diets are delivered at the client's doorstep. It is the first in the city so we have the edge. We help people lose weight in a healthy way and some clients with medical condition, and all of them have benefitted from our program. We are counseling them on healthy lifestyle and making healthy food choices. I wouldn't ask for more since I'm doing the things I love the most: cooking and proper nutrition.

Next year, we will start a deal to provide post workout meals to clients of a famous crossfit gym in our city and we are all excited for this new opportunity that is also another way of fulfilling my passion! I can finally see the fruits of my labor. Everything was like planned out for me to get here and in God's perfect time!

Currently, my husband and I am all occupied with our businesses and with our handful 15- month old son, Matthew, who I still exclusively breastfeed up until now. I guess, turning into healthy living at the same time living my passion will not only benefit me but also the people around me. As my name implies, this woman right here is "on fire" to be an advocate of good health and proper nutrition. Juggling the business, being a wife and a full time mom is not easy but I am grateful to God because I am blessed!

> "The way to achieve your own success is to be willing to help somebody else get it first."
> — Iyanla Vanzant

Gaby McEwan Bio

Gaby McEwan and her husband Rodney started Remax, My Property Group in 2015 and believes that PEOPLE are more important than property.

Gaby writes a weekly blog "The Real Deal" and is also an author. She has 2 teenagers, 2 dogs and 2 cats – although she argues that one of the cats is actually a human.

The Real Deal

Gaby McEwan – Australia

After many years of working in radio, I went into real estate. I was tired of being inside a studio all day. When you are in radio, everyone wants to know you and be on your show. I was a bit disappointed to see real estate agents are regarded with far less enthusiasm than radio announcers.

When I started in real estate I had no help or support at all and I often wonder how many good people slip through the system. I set off to a great start and sold three properties in the first 6 weeks. Then I hit a wall.

When I had my first slump I talked to two male colleagues expecting encouragement. They both agreed I should leave as I was a mother to two young boys and a wife and I should be with my family.

Something made me tenacious and I hung on – I think it was because they saw something in me they were afraid of. It was a bit of a boy's club back then and there weren't too many young women with families selling property. I used to bring my boys (on occasion) to listing appointments. They became very savvy about pricing property and I used to often use them in my photoshoots of lifestyle property and even dress them up!

Working in real estate is a series of valleys and mountains. You grow more in the difficult times when you have to dig deep than in any other times.

Of course, there have been mountain-tops too, like selling multi-million dollar properties and each sale gives me great happiness. I thrive on serving people and helping them move on from their current situation. There are sometimes unhappy circumstances behind a sale, and you need to show compassion and empathy. You also need to help people to navigate this journey.

It is a privilege to serve others.

I've worked through challenging times in the last ten years – selling in the worst market on the Sunshine Coast (2011-2013) when most properties had dropped in value by around 15-20%.

Moving to Brisbane was the best decision we made. I was fortunate enough to meet a developer before I left at a volunteer's dinner and he reluctantly took a punt on me and gave me 7 blocks of land to sell. With no advertising and sheer hard work I sat at the blocks night and day and sold them all in 10 days. These 7 blocks of land have turned into over 80 and enabled me to start my own business from scratch, My Property Group.

In fact, one of the first people I announced my crazy idea to was Nikki Taylor and she was incredibly encouraging. I held on to this gift of encouragement and it meant the world to me! Encouragers are awesome – be one.

My best business decision was to recruit my husband who has been successful in his businesses and also corporate life (he was National Specifications manager of Zip Heaters across Australia and had a team under him).

He started a rent roll from scratch and it is so good to work alongside him. He runs the office and rent roll – and I focus on the sales side of the business.

On a personal note, my mantra are the words: "All things are possible to those who believe". It takes belief and a lot of action to succeed at anything.

Since initially contributing to this inspiring website, an opportunity came up to buy a Real Estate office which had then been established for over 17 years and started by a wonderful couple, Ron and Lenore Sieber who are very well known and respected in Brisbane, Australia. How I came to buy it is another story for another day. The legacy I want to leave behind in this world is to ENCOURAGE others and also to ENCOURAGE business people to be GENEROUS.

People think "when I've got enough I will give".

Give today. Don't wait. Choose what is important to you and work backwards. You can't give to others when you are no longer here! There are so many children that need to be sponsored. Don't look at the millions. Start with just one. That was what Mother Theresa taught us.

My father came to each of his children before he died and gave us some money. He said "I want to see you enjoy it whilst I am alive." His grandfather did the same and he was able to buy his first car at a young age. My father (Edward Bowen-Jones) was the most generous person I ever knew. He was a brilliant surgeon yet spent a lot of his life operating on people that couldn't afford to pay him.

I am so proud that my two boys have learnt to be generous. My eldest son is just so kind and exudes this wonderful level of service and amazing work ethic.

My youngest son recently went to India to play cricket and they were all encouraged to be generous by the coaches. He donated some of his cricket kit to the very talented but disadvantaged young boys he met. He even gave up his new spikes as one of the boys had sores under his feet as his shoes had worn out. This made my heart sing!

I think too often in life we hold back, when the Earth was created – think about it, we didn't get given ONE shade of pink for flowers. There's such an incredible variation. There's not even only one species of zebra. There's the mountain Zebra and the Burchell Zebra. They both have different stripe patterns.

Nature is generous, extravagant; it replaces itself and there is NO lack. Wherever you look you see abundance. Each dawn is new and fresh and full of promise.

> "I'd rather regret the things I've done than regret the things I haven't done."
> Lucille Ball

Phillippa Jacobs Bio

In 1997, Phillippa founded Pinnacle Design Limited. With also naming her business Mega Advertising for 10 years, she found it important to refocus the company direction and in 2017 has rebranded to Pinnacle & Co. Limited, to represent the peak of Christchurch's creative design talent.

Pinnacle went from strength to strength backed by the success of our clients. The Pinnacle team worked with businesses of all shapes and sizes across a variety of industries, providing wonderful websites, creative designs, effective strategic advertising campaigns and all manner of marketing material.

Pinnacle's strength and ability to help partner their clients has really thrived. With a stronger brand and focus on strategy has lead them to offering creative ideas and planned solutions, with a reach that expanded well past Christchurch to all of New Zealand and Australia.

What Defines Someone Who Is Inspirational?

Phillippa Jacobs – New Zealand

What defines someone as inspirational? To me it means inspiring others to step up too by doing the walking, not just the talking.

My business is Pinnacle & Co. Limited in Christchurch, New Zealand. I started Pinnacle in 1997. This hasn't happened by luck or by mistake. Nor has it by blood sweat or tears. Okay, I lie, a few tears!!! It has happened with passion, and dedication, and a lot of laughs too.

I started as a first class honours visual communications student looking for work. It didn't take long to get work but the next few months proved pretty tough.

I had been fired for glandular fever, fired for severely hurting my knee (4 surgeries), made redundant twice, terminated with wrong contract, you get the picture. Then major self doubt set in with government interviews (in order to claim a financial benefit). They suggested that perhaps I wasn't very good at design (forgetting I have first class honours). I was determined to get a job, and a good one!

I hit the pavement over and over visiting what now are only describe as our oppositions, until an amazing man Terry Kearns offered me rent free for six months at his advertising studio, to start my own business. My CV was looking pretty bad, so I talked with my parents, even though I was only age 26 and we thought "why not!"

So December 12th, 1997 was a day I've never looked back on. It taught me anything is possible, even with low self esteem at High School and not a good start into a career path. I learned that to believe in yourself was the first magic step. And when someone tells you can do it, believe that they just could be right. There will always be people that can't do what I've done, but I believe all people have potential to do their best, and that is how I live each day, with my glass half full attitude.

I have a truly wonderful team of staff. They are very loyal and supportive, hard working and clever. I believe what Richard Branson says, be good to your staff and they will be good to your clients (and you)! So true. They are good to me, which in turn makes me love my workplace too. If you love your job then it shows in your work and your life!

So how do I inspire people when it seems to me that what I do is just normal? Yet weekly, if not daily, I cross paths with someone that says how much I inspire them. It's crazy at times; people who inspire me are often the ones that say I inspire them. Awesome. I guess it comes to another common saying: hang out with successful people and you too will be successful. I add to that with happiness too. I need happy people round me to be happy! I thrive on people being nice to other people.

We love helping small/medium businesses succeed. Yes, we help many large national and international businesses too, but it is the businesses where there are less hoops to jump through, no politics, just passion to succeed that we have the most success with – because they let us drive them. Pure excitement.

So what do I do? I go to work each day. I do have good holidays but when I am at work, I work, because I want to. Because I enjoy watching my company make others so happy. I'm still motivated to take my business further. I don't need it to be the biggest, but I do need it to be the best!!!

The other part of making my world better, is what I am able to do for everyone else. There is something special about helping other people. As a person, and as a business we do so much for charity work. I belong to Zonta, I run a youth group for Zonta (Z Club) at Avonside Girls' High School. I chair *Kiwi Business Chicks*, since 2006, I have been a member of BNI since 2005, I am on the Industries Board at *Yoobee School of Design*. And at *Pinnacle* we do a host of different things to help charities do better.

Why? The values that I have had instilled in me, are the values I wish to spread to others. My personal values come through in my business as we love helping businesses, we love helping people. Our clients love our openness our friendliness, and this is what gets me up in the morning to do more in our world.

We are always growing our own business as well, we are proud to be Strategic Creative Partners with our amazing clients.

"Just don't give up trying to do what you really want to do. Where there is love and inspiration, I don't think you can go wrong."
Ella Fitzgerald

Maz Schirmer Bio

Maz is an expert in the psychology of Women's Success, an author of The MAZ Factor, Founder of Institute of Women International, Innovator of Creatrix® and Head Trainer and Licensor of Creatrix® Facilitators in 6 countries and expanding rapidly.

She is a mother of 4 and a Nana of 9 living in Sunshine Coast, Australia. She's a woman on a mission with a passion and a vision to release suppression from an entire gender.

Why 1000 Self Help Books Won't Set Women Fully Free. Discover the MAZ Factor

Maz Schirmer – Australia

I WAS WORTH AS MUCH AS THE CHEWING GUM BENEATH THE SHOES OF MEN.

That was the level of my self-worthiness that caused my life for 3 decades to be of terror, torment and turbulence. I'm not just talking about the rape, injustice and abuse by men that led to myself and my 4 little kids having to go live in hiding for more than 400 days. I'm talking about the self-inflicted abuse upon myself because of my lack of self-worth.

I was simply living my mother's and her mother's life, not to mention 1 of my daughters experienced the same. What's the chances of not just having 4 generations of women with guns at our heads in my family by men, but for myself, by several men. DV and child sexual abuse was rampant in my genes. I knew it was a pattern when my own 3 daughters were molested, yet I was going to be the one who NEVER let that happen to my kids. Well merely wanting to be a changemaker is not enough, in fact the full on focus of that subject is what kept the pattern alive.

Well the mind image I produced by 'not' wanting my kids to experience abuse meant my image was of my kids being abused. The writing was on the wall and I had no idea i was a life creation artist. I had no idea the power of my own mind and how our mind images create our reality.

Suppression issues that currently show up as 'not good enough', anxiety, depression and self-loathing (sometimes disguised with a confidence mask) are not just ours, we inherited them, or at least the predisposition for events to occur to us that sustain our own suppression.

I finally told myself that I'd start a new life by blacking out my past. Well I blacked out alright, on the floor in a phone box while fleeing yet again into emergency housing, when I woke up from my first ever epileptic fit. In that 'bleep' moment when I first awoke, before my beliefs, conditioning and past memories caught up with me, was this moment of pure clarity that triggered a decision that went on to shape the rest of my life.

I saw it was MY responsibility to break this cycle because we were lucky to be alive and wouldn't be if I kept making similar choices. I really turned my life around on a dime because of that bleep moment!

I went from an unemployed check out 'chick' single mother of 4 on the sole parent pension, living in emergency housing without a passport, to becoming the number 1 women's business leader of other women in business, within 10 countries after being told it couldn't be done. I broke Aussie 43 year records that I still own today.

Well that was well and good, but after a decade and a half of living the 5 star life, cruising the world on Moet, taking 26 overseas trips (in just 14 years), I can tell you that money is great, but it is not soul fulfilling when you see the statistics first hand of the numbers that fail compared to the numbers who succeed to their own definition of success as entrepreneurs.

I decided to focus on creating a REAL solution that would stop so many women feeling life failures at business and life.

I realised that in business we were ALL teaching processes that made me secretly feel like I was a fraud, a fluke and ashamed because I was NOT consistent. I DIDN'T plan my work and work my plan, I didn't even set goals, therefore I wasn't practicing what I was preaching. I was teaching these strategies because I was taught to by the 'GREATS' who said that's how it's done. Luckily for 1 in 5 these strategies worked well, but not for the 4/5.

I'd stumbled on the WOMAN'S success formula and didn't know it. After all every self-help book said that's the way to achieve success so who was I to speak otherwise.

One day it dawned on me. Why am I listening to these men (male company managers, male guru's and male authors of the biggest selling self-help books and seminars) tell me how to do it when I had years and years of EVIDENCE saying OTHERWISE.

That was my second LIFE DEFINING MOMENT. That's what led me to launch the INSTITUTE OF WOMEN INTERNATIONAL and formulate Creatrix®, a woman's breakthrough process that breaks the cycle of suppression.

My mission now is to SET 10 MILLION WOMEN'S HEARTS AND MINDS FREE.

We are the solution we've been waiting for. We know what's good for us and need to trust that! We can achieve ANYTHING when we break the cycle.

> "The question isn't who's going to let me; it's who is going to stop me."
> Ayn Rand

> **Julie Sawchuk Bio**
>
> Julie Sawchuk is a wife, mother of two, teacher, athlete and author. As a person with a disability she is working to change people's ideas about accessibility, road safety and perseverance. She shares her ideas on her blog, as a speaker to schools and through the media. Julie's blog "Living life with Paralysis" can be read at <u>www.juliesawchuk.blogspot.ca</u>.

Life can Change in the Blink of an Eye!

Julie Sawchuk – Canada

They say that life can change in the blink of an eye. There is no better example than what happened to me on July 29th 2015. I live in Huron County, on the "west coast" of Ontario, Canada where endurance athletes ski in the wintertime and swim, bike and run in the summer. On this particularly beautiful day while out on a 60 km training ride I was hit from behind by a car traveling at full speed. Thrown into the ditch, I sustained multiple life threatening injuries, including a T4 spinal cord injury that left me with paralysis from the chest down. I was forced from my two wheels on to the four wheels of my wheelchair – for the rest of my life. I spent 10 days in hospital and three months in rehabilitation – away from my friends and family. It was lonely, but necessary, as I had to learn how to live with my new body. In rehab I started to rebuild my strength and endurance and learn how to handle a bladder and bowels that did not function properly.

The local media covered my story because I had close ties to many parts of this small community. I was a secondary school science teacher and Nordic ski coach and had a close group of triathlon training friends. I spoke to the media about road safety and, with the help of my community, we started the Huron County Share the Road campaign.

Our bumper stickers can be seen across Huron County and around the province. I also started to write a blog, to give my brain an outlet, a way to stop questions of the future from spinning around in my head. Now I write for lots of reasons.

Sharing my story has become a top priority for me – a way of reaching out to others in similar situations. I found that there was not a lot of guidance available to me, so I wanted others to benefit from the knowledge I had gained so far. As an educator I never like to miss an opportunity and I had learned that many people did not know what it was like to live with paralysis. I decided that the best thing would be to share it all. And so I do – I have written more than 100 posts that have been read by thousands of people. I write about paralysis, accessibility in our built environment, fitness and sport, relationships, driving, travel, kids, frustrations, chronic pain and depression. It has not been easy. My life, my family and my relationships have all changed.

When I left rehab I was told I had a 12% chance of recovering. So that has been my focus – twelve is not zero – and the only way to know is to try. It will not happen "just like that" it will take a lot of work. So that is what I do. I work on my body trying to make it move again. Physiotherapy four days a week, plus exercises at home, and it's working. I have abdominal, back and hip flexor muscles that are responding. The hard work is paying off. Not only that, I am also hearing from people who are following my story, people who have been inspired to push through the difficulty that they face in their own lives. Because, let's face it, everyone has adversity at some time or another, mine is just a bit more obvious when I roll up to greet you. Ernest Hemingway said it best: *"Now is no time to think of what you do not have. Think of what you can do with what there is."*

> ### Liz la Force Bio
>
> Liz has been born with a strong intuition and ability to heal. She has learnt to communicate with body, mind and soul. Through this atonement Liz is able to understand the processes that are going on in a human or organization and can guide them towards their authentic true self.
>
> Liz has learnt most by experience, but has also a degree in business economics, Chinese medicine, diverse healing methods, and teaching. Nowadays her work is mainly focused on teaching. With her new company Get Real she organizes retreats, and workshops. For business, adults, kids and parents and lovers.

A Strong Intuition and Ability to Heal

Liz La Force – Ibiza

When does one start to awaken…the moment we are born or the moment we realize we are not what we think we are. Our body, our mind, our emotion, our personality.

For me this moment came quite early at the age of 10 I already started to ask my mother about the purpose of life here on earth. An answer that she at that moment could not provide to me.

An answer I would start to search for from age 24 when I totally collapsed and was bed bound for two years. A blessing in disguise as many traumatic and/or life changing experiences often are.

Since nobody could heal me, although I tried almost every medicine, both regular and alternative, I was "forced" to heal myself. And so I did. It took me 13 years to heal my illness. A wonderful journey back to my true self.

It was a interesting journey, one which taught me a huge lesson. As a light worker I am very fond, like many of us, of the light. But I learnt along the way that we are both light and dark. To truly heal or become whole again, we need to look into the face of our demons. Which is not always easy, but very worthwhile. Since they are there it is good to know, understand and learn how to love them. So they can start to work for you instead of against you. You meaning your true self.

Along the way I reconnected with my healing gifts and I learnt how to use and deepen them. Mostly by inner guidance and sometimes through spiritual masters that I met. After a world travel I was guided to Ibiza in 2014, a small island in the mediterranean sea. Since then I have been working on and from this magical island.

My life has even more expanded since then. It is all about being able to open our heart to receive the gifts life is offering us, day in day out – no exceptions. We just need to recognize the gifts. Because sometimes they come in a package that is different than we expected.

Since my life is so much overflowing with gifts it feels only natural to share them with others. And I am very happy to be able to do so on a daily basis. With love, gratitude and dedication I go further on my journey. Knowing that there is still so much more to experience.

Deborah Johnston Bio

Deborah Johnston is a Well Being Mentor, Entrepreneur, Conqueror of Cancer, Published Co-Author and at present is also writing her very first Book, all about getting and having Courage! These days after learning many cathartic things about life, she has an innate calling, and feel it is her sole duty and purpose to work with women, as their personal confidante` Mentor, passing on and sharing what she knows about life, in all of its textures, colours, challenges and joys!

Working with women, just like you, who have a deep yearning to achieve "more" from life! Guiding you, step by step to create the life that you SO deserve to have, the life that you want SO badly, that NEW YOU that wants to make some changes!

Living Life Positively Courageous, with Femininity & Style!

Deborah Johnston – Australia

After a diagnosis of terminal abdominal cancer in 2005 and being told by my Oncologist I had to "get my things in order", as I only had 6 months to live, I am sitting here writing this article for you, 11 years later in 2017, feeling very alive and well and reflecting on everything that I went through to lead me to this point.

When you get news as shattering as that, it changes your perspective on life forever, it rocks you to your core being, and nothing is ever the same after that.

I was carrying a very heavy load of grief, after a Miscarriage, a failed Romance, losing both Parents to Cancer, and dealing with bullying in the workplace, and Retrenchment from my Corporate Job in Recruitment.

So, how did I get through all of that you may be wondering? Honestly, sometimes I ask myself the very same question. Sometimes I shake my head in disbelief that I am still here living and breathing to tell my story. Sometimes I pinch myself, sometimes it feels surreal.

In basic terms, I simply said NO to Chemotherapy & Radiation – it was that simple. I carefully chose a Natural approach to getting well and positive results came my way. I was well informed and with the support of my wonderful GP, I did my Research on my options to heal myself naturally – so that's what I did.

From a mindset perspective, my healing involved learning to dig very deeply inside myself to find the courage and hope to keep on going. Opening up my self-awareness, and owning it, was so cathartic and it worked tenfold.

By journaling and meditating and asking for a "Medical Miracle" and doing all sorts of things I loved, to raise my spirit and self-belief and self-esteem. The most cathartic turning point for me to let go of my painful past and choose to "change", came when I began studying Human Behaviour and NLP-Neuro Linguistic Programming and surrounding myself with positive like-minded people and successful Entrepreneurs and Mentors. Who to this day still encourage and support my quest to inspire people with my story, and beyond that with my Mentoring Business and being a Guest Speaker at Events.

Gaining a Masters in NLP & Neurological Re-Patterning– was certainly the most empowering thing I have ever done and certainly the most profound and effective method I have ever come across to heal at a deep Neurological level. Which I share with my Mentoring Clients and in my Workshops and Retreats.

I feel it is my quest and purpose in life now, to inspire women, and I am smiling widely with gratitude to be alive and breathing, and being able to share my story with you!

I am thrilled to say I am currently writing my first Book, *"Absolutely Courageous" – 10 Steps To Finding Courage When You Are Stretched To Your Limits* – which will be Published later in 2017. A goal I have had for over 20 years is coming to fruition!

Having goals and ambition and knowing what your passions are in life, and following them are very important aspects to know about yourself.

I learned this early on in life from my inspiring Mother who had a very successful Business when I was a Teenager. It propels you forward into the future, and paves the way to manifest what you really want from your precious life!

Gratitude is something I practise daily, it's a powerful force to be reckoned with, lean into it, embrace it easily by being grateful for what you do have. Gratitude will shift your mood – practise Gratitude daily and repeat every morning, and notice how your life changes.

Mine has! Yours can too!

Life's for Living Positively Courageous, Feminine & Stylish!

"Do you really want to look back on your life and see how wonderful it could have been had you not been afraid to live it?"

Caroline Myss

> **Pauleanna Reid Bio**
>
> Pauleanna Reid is a Motivational Speaker, Millennial Mentor, Celebrity/CEO Ghostwriter and critically acclaimed Author of her fiction novel, "Everything I Couldn't Tell My Mother". Through a whirlwind of inspirational lectures, round table discussions and media appearances she positively influences, challenges and reconnects youth with their passions. Pauleanna uses incredible wit and candor to empower women and girls.

Push Past Your Limits
Pauleanna Reid - Canada

If you had told my teenaged self that I would be a mentor, motivational speaker, best-selling author and multi-business owner before the age of 30, I wouldn't have believed you. The journey to becoming the woman I am now, a woman who goes after she wants and won't take no for an answer, has been anything but easy.

My adolescence was marked by bullying, low self-esteem and unhappiness. I found solace in writing. I eventually realized it could be a career for me. But I was failing English and my teachers told me it would never happen. My parents push me to choose a "safe" career. I was surrounded by naysayers.

So I went to college for a program chosen by my parents. I was deeply unhappy with my life. I hated school, I hated my program, and I hated that I was only sticking through it because it was what other people expected for me. I fell into a deep depression, barely able to hold it together. On the day of my final exam, the only thing standing between me and graduation, I stood up, tore up my test paper, walked out of the exam room and never looked back.

It was the most terrifying thing I've ever done, but it was my moment of liberation. I sought help for my depression and found mentors who guided me in developing my career as a nationally-published journalist. By the age of 22, I had bylines in major news publications across Canada. I had established the same career my naysayers had told me I could never have.

A few years later, I fulfilled another dream of mine, penning my first novel, "Everything I Couldn't Tell My Mother." Writing my novel was really an act of catharsis for me. I saw it as an opportunity to address that emotional baggage I'd been carrying and begin my healing process. My book also helped me to start a real conversation with my mother and tell her the secrets I'd been holding in for years. But "Everything I Couldn't Tell My Mother" was also for all the women who could understand where I'd been. I wanted to give them a story that would empower them as much as it empowered me.

That's my ultimate goal in everything I do. I want to always be able to give others the opportunity to see beyond the limits of their circumstances. That's why my proudest accomplishment to date is New Girl on the Block, a mentorship program for millennial women in transition. I started the mentorship program two years ago in collaboration with my business partner, Safia Bartholomew. Together, we've helped over 100 mentees in six countries take their distant dreams and turn them into noteworthy achievements.

It's truly the greatest contribution I could make with my life. To be able to work directly with other young people and offer them the support and guidance to help them see that 'impossible is nothing' is the fuel that keeps me going every day. It's what gets me out of bed at 4:30 every morning. It's what allows me to own and operate three businesses and work a full-time job I love.

H.D. Thoreau once said, "If a person advances confidently in the direction of his dreams and lives life fully, then he will find success in unexpected hours." I live by this. Regardless of the limitations I face or the naysayers that try to discourage me, I always keep pushing for what I want. It's something that I encourage every woman to do; proceed without permission, push past your limits, and forget the haters.

Suzie Lightfoot Bio

Suzie Lightfoot is a Mother, Business Owner, Media Personality, Fashion Identity, Keynote Speaker, Personal Brand Expert, who understands the complexities of what it takes to make it to the top as a professional woman in her 40's.

After 25 years in the corporate world as a business owner, brand ambassador, top international model and professional athlete, Suzie has the real-life "know how" to help other professional women package themselves to get to the top.

Suzie helps professional women develop strong Personal Brands that re-energize them and position them as leaders in both life and business so that they can have more choices, more opportunities and more financial security.

Why Your Story Matters

Suzie Lightfoot – Australia

Let me just start by saying, I love being a woman, and I love what I do! However, everyone knows that being a woman in business doesn't come without its challenges!

I believe everything that happens in our life we can learn and prosper from. Even heartbreak, loss and failure. Every challenge or moment of adversity gives an elevation of thought and tests your passion. They shape us into who we are today. In fact, interpreting your experiences with adversity and failure can be an exciting way to change your future.

My journey started as an elite athlete at the Australian Institute of Sport, where I learned the foundations of leadership, personal drive, focus and the power of self-confidence and visualisation. Now I share these success rituals with other women so that they can achieve extraordinary goals too.

I've enjoyed success as a model, media personality, brand ambassador and businesswoman and for the past 25 years, I've worked with industry leaders in media, PR, marketing and brand leadership.

I've also worked with some of the biggest names in fashion, learning first-hand how a simple piece of fabric can empower a person and alter people's perceptions.

But it hasn't always been a smooth road to success. As a single mum and business woman for over 20 years, I had certainly experienced extreme highs and terrible lows, including two broken marriages, brushes with depression, workplace bullying and sexual harassment at a time when my life and 'public' image appeared perfect from the outside. These experiences, although so painful, emotionally exhausting and challenging at the time, ultimately laid the foundations for my new business and success I have achieved today.

For me, my biggest aha moment was when I turned 50. After fighting back from years of feeling invisible and insecure, I finally got the courage to quit my job and back myself in my new business! I had found a niche that I deeply connected and resonated with. Helping other professional women in their 40's turn their life experiences into powerful personal brands so that they have more choices, attract more opportunities and can be more financially secure. It's a role that I love, I am passionate about, and is a natural extension of who I am and all that I've accomplished in my career.

I believe that acknowledging your personal story and journey is so important in your plan for success. So many of us look back at moments in our lives and wonder how on earth did we managed to be so fearless in our pursuit of success. When we're young, we naturally feel invincible, but that can fade as we age. We find that we no longer fit into the 'square' we are in and we have a growing fear for financial security. We also lack the courage to put ourselves 'out there' in today's professional landscape, that values youthful dewy complexions over experience and know-how.

Taking a moment to look back on your story and all that you have achieved and experienced in life, personally and professionally, can help you to reboot your self- confidence. It changes your perspective and transforms the way that you view yourself today. Your personal journey is all part of your unique story! It's your foundation that shapes and defines your true values and beliefs and is the cornerstone of building your authentic personal brand. Your personal brand is your unique real-world fingerprint and digital footprint. All will recognise it. No-one will replicate it.

Shifting your mindset and attitude can make all the difference when you're faced with failure, loss of confidence, or challenging moments in both life and business. In fact, the one thing that all successful people have in common is the ability to refresh and reboot their mindset and to power on and turn their biggest failures into their greatest success.

Highs and lows are all part of your journey to success. They make you more resilient, determined and strong. In fact, failure is not the end, it's just the beginning!

Today I am on a mission to change the conversation about women and aging in the workplace. I am driven to help other professional women walk into a room and just own it. No apologies, no hiding, no holding back. I believe in speaking the truth about who you really are. Success is a choice. The future is ahead of you. You can be whatever you want to be!

"Whatever you do, be different – that was the advice my mother gave me, and I can't think of better advice for an entrepreneur. If you're different, you will stand out."
Anita Roddick

Nikki Taylor Bio

I am inspired with absolute passion and energy to assist in changing the lives of many humans with mentoring and assisting others in their careers, I am the proud founder of *REJS, MVAT* and *Be Inspired – Inspiring Women Today*.

I continue to be inspired everyday by the amazing people around me. My vision to start Inspiring Women today was to find as many women around the globe to tell their very own stories, share their successes and this is how Be Inspired was born.

I am a wife, mother, stepmother, grandmother, aunty, niece and sister in law and cousin and friend and mentor to many.

As an entrepreneur, my experiences in building my own businesses and working in the Recruitment industry, Headhunting industry and mentoring has always sparked a passion for sharing Inspiring Women Today, globally. I will continue to share these amazing stories because we all have a life waiting to be lived, and a story waiting to be told.

Part of loving life and enjoying it every day is leading a lifestyle where working anywhere, in any location, no office and being cubicle or office free is my norm. My office goes with me wherever I go, it is 100% mobile, 100% virtual and 100% paperless! Working smarter than ever before doing what I love but also by working smarter this means that I have a work/life balance to be proud of – and so can you!

There is no magic bullet or instant formula for success – you can make it simple. Find what you love to do. Work smarter at it and get help when you need it.

I've found mine. What's yours?

Freedom Lifestyle – Don't Hold Me Back
Nikki Taylor – Australia

With an absolute passion for life and working as a Talent and Headhunting Specialist I have managed to create that elusive work/life balance that everyone is searching for, don't get me wrong, I still work incredibly hard in a very demanding industry, I get to do it my way though, that's all. I also believe that there is always a fabulous story about every single one of us whether good or bad. The best thing is we can learn from our mistakes and choose what NOT to do next time.

After only three years in the Recruitment industry I took the bold step and ventured out on my own and started my very own recruitment company, yes, this has had its challenges, however, there have been more rewards along the way as well, mostly in the form of awesome happy candidates getting their dream positions. The idea of working in any corporate office did not align with me. I just didn't belong even as an employee I was always that one person that stood out and did not like the rules.

Every single day I learn something new and I really love what I do with a passion no matter what it is I'm putting my heart and soul into. Why you may ask do I do what I do?

In the beginning I was told as a recruiter in a National New Zealand recruitment a company that I could not recruit in the Real Estate industry, that was the day I knew I had to do it myself. I went with the Richard Branson theory – "screw it just do it". My absolute ah-ha moment. I never felt the fit was right for me when, as an employee there were too many rules. I went out to design my own brand in New Zealand and run my own recruitment business, different to the rest.

In 2009, this was the year that I "sold" my successful recruitment company in New Zealand to make the move to Australia. This wasn't the easiest process to go through and a hurdle I wouldn't wish upon any business. What I can say is the entire experience made me a stronger and more determined person to not let a setback get in the way of my success. It was a moment that one would either give up or get up and continue to show up.

Today I would thank the horrid event for making me stronger. Without going into the messy details and with the best legal advice in the world, I still lost everything. It taught me about trust and my absolute takeaway from it today was get up show up make it happen no matter what the event and that's what I did. Yes there was a big financial loss and we had already moved to Australia, there wasn't much I could change at the time but I came out with so much in personal gain as a person and this made me more resolute to do better next time and not take too much on trust and face value.

We arrived in Australia in 2009, started a new Recruitment Specialist company for the Real Estate industry, no clients, no candidates, no database, actually nothing! I had my mobile phone, desktop and clunky old laptop computer and THE most amazing attitude that I had to make it happen. Determined to create a lifestyle around work and run a company nationally, all virtual. Now, the brand is a well recognised National recruitment company.

Those who know me well know that I ooze energy from 5am to 9pm, a non-stop go getter, yes I crash at the end of the day and I'm always grateful for an amazing day after I have had the chance to talk to fabulous people and an opportunity to change their lives in whatever I do. I have been known as a can fizzy shaken up.

I'm known to be in a cafe anytime between 5am and 7am no matter the season, weather or location. My best planning times and creative moments happen in those two hours.

As I am writing this very story, I have taken another risk by selling our Gold Coast apartment, created a minimalist lifestyle, placed all our furniture into storage and started the road trip with no address, no time frame as such with locations being a surprise from month to month.

Working from locations we haven't stayed at, I have set up a virtual office at each destination and intend to do this for about 6 to 12 months, but hey who knows what will happen! Can you imagine how many people we are meeting, staying in Airbnb accommodations, with an absolute goal to run my businesses on the road and continue to create and grow personally.

As you can see, I love what I do – I speak that lingo every day, I tell myself everyday that I'm grateful for everything I have and love to help others in anyway. That's why I love what I do with absolute passion. I am daily seen on Social Media platforms working virtual with my man, my bestie and my business partner. We are always travelling and working interstate and overseas and always seen daily working in a non-office environment. Freedom Lifestyle – Don't Hold Me Back.

Tina's Banitska Bio

Tina studied fine arts at Melbourne University, Victoria Australia and postgraduate sculpting at RMIT, before she was employed as an art consultant in Ballarat in the late 1970s. But it was while she was operating her Creswick Springmount Pottery, opened in 1981 and which she still operates today, that she had a vision for the historic 19th century mansion.

I Never Lost Sight Of What I Wanted To Do

Tina Banitska – Australia

It's the story of how, in the late 1970s, sculptor Tina Banitska drove into Daylesford, spied the tower of the Holy Cross Convent and declared to her friend: "One day, that is going to be one of Australia's best galleries."

A decade later, with barely any finances but a powerful sense of destiny being fulfilled, she took a massive loan to purchase the empty, crumbling building. In the subsequent two years of renovation and delay, due to money and all manner of issues – Tina sold many of her treasured possessions in order to pay tradie wages, opening in 1991 on the day the banks vowed to foreclose the project.

Tina went through an enormous personal and professional struggle with not only her bank balance but her reputation at stake as well. She overcame so many obstacles along her way that would have led many people of lesser character and drive to just quit …. and walk away.

Since opening way back in 1991 the gallery has now doubled in size, it now attracts over 200,000 visitors a year to its art-filled rooms, the cafe, the museum and the gardens – all the while continuing to service bank loans – underscores her true legend.

But the personal story of Tina, her philanthropy and her vision for the future of rural Victorian art, is less known.

Wiping away tears, Tina – who on most days is an intensely private person despite her bubbliness – recounts the story of what has been her underlying driver at the Convent.

"Success for me is not about money or what you achieve. It's about how you follow a dream, pursuing things your heart tells you is important," she says. "I've never seen this as a sacrifice. It's been a huge blessing."

Her greatest driving force, she says, was her impoverished childhood. The daughter of Greek migrants, her most vivid memories are of her hard-working, generous parents, Steve and Sophia, whom she now looks after. "I remember my mother, I would have been four or five, holding my hand and saying she had a shilling and should she spend it on vegetables or bread," says Tina.

"It wasn't about money, but choices, the decisions you make. That memory has never gone away. It makes me feel how everything is possible. It's not about the barriers that stop you but where your heart is. Money is just a vehicle."

"When I heard it was for sale, all I could imagine was artists working together. I could picture it. I couldn't sleep for two months, I'd wake with hot and cold sweats, I was very unsettled until I got it," she says. "I do believe in energies beyond what we understand. I think there was a plan somewhere for this."

But when she took possession Tina admits she "cried for hours and hours", such was the derelict state of the building, built in the 1860s. Yet she "never lost sight of what I wanted to do".

"Even when I had a loan of $1.5 million at 18.5 per cent locked-in interest rates for five years it didn't deter me." When the Convent Gallery finally opened on March 31, 1991 – the same day the banks were set to foreclose – there were 5052 customers. "But we didn't have an entrance fee and we didn't have anything to sell," she recalls.

In 2001 Tina borrowed more, nearly $3 million, to double the size of the gallery, incorporating a chapel and school, and now function rooms. Never has she applied for a grant.

Looking back she admits those early years "don't seem real", with her average day now spent as an "office girl", working up to 14 hours with customers or cleaning toilets. While not religious, she categorises herself as spiritual, believing in the "goodness and kindness of humans".

"I've been given the privilege of looking after this building, to make it a place for the community. I don't own anything, I'm the custodian of it," she says. "It was all in the plan. I was just given the strength, courage, foresight and planning to make it happen."

Tina's greatest love is mentoring young people. She estimates she has taken hundreds of budding artists under her wing over the years – dancers, fashion designers, jewellers, painters, not just locals but international exchanges as well.

"This job is about people, it's one of the reasons I set the Convent up, to share and interact and engage people," says Tina, who has owned and sold several galleries in rural Victoria.

"Art is the only inspiration we have to keep our hope going. It uplifts the spirit."

"Optimism is the faith that leads to achievement."
Helen Keller

Zahrina Robertson Bio

Zahrina Robertson is a leading international multi-award winning personal branding photographer and video strategist. She is also a speaker and the author of NEW BOOK *"Magnetic Branding - The Complete Guide For A Brand That Attracts!"*

Magnetic Branding

Zahrina Robertson – Australia

For Zahrina Robertson taking photos is deeply personal. From the moment she picked up a camera as a child, exploring the beauty and simplicity of the world around her, she was hooked. Born into a home where cameras had pride of place, Zahrina took up photography as not only a way to make a living but as her way of making a difference in people's lives. Inspired by her father, who was an amateur photographer, she was in awe of his ability to take every day things and transform them.

Fast-forward to now, and her passion for photography and connecting with others is what sets her apart. For Zahrina, photography is not a job; it is an extension of her psyche and her heart. It gives back and feeds her soul by allowing her to tap into her creativity. Her gift behind the lens, coupled with her passion for personal branding, sees her create photos that have people going 'WOW'.

There is no 'point and shoot' in Zahrina's studio. She doesn't just do headshots; she is a maverick magician who makes people's personal branding irresistible. The journey to creating an entrepreneur's personal brand starts even before Zahrina picks up a camera. Her genius is in transforming people – helping them to really think about their brand, their business messages, how they can do things differently – and ultimately capturing their x-factor.

Zahrina's gift personifies the saying 'a picture is worth a thousand words'. She understands that an image defines a person's brand and believes that those first few seconds are vital, especially for 21st-century entrepreneurs. The image has to tell a story, to capture the heart and soul, and to engage the viewer so they see the 'real' person they are about to do business with.

As a keynote speaker, Zahrina's authenticity is one of her greatest assets. She has the ability to take people with her every step of the way as she demystifies the complex world of branding – ensuring that they truly understand how to do it better, and the value of getting it right. Honest, funny and quirky, Zahrina leaves her audiences secure in the knowledge that she knows her stuff and that she has imparted valuable information to help them create razor sharp branding. Her wisdom and insights on how to use imagery to connect with clients see her regularly approached by the media and businesses who want to stand out and be noticed.

Zahrina has photographed such international entrepreneurs as Ita Buttrose, Tim Ferris, Taki Moore, Matt Church and Dale Beaumont. She has also covered events featuring Richard Branson, Martha Stewart, George Clooney and stars of the music industry such as Dannii Minogue.

Street smart, savvy and classy, Zahrina is a multi-award winning photographer and a Telstra Business Woman of the Year nominee. After a whirlwind five years she has expanded her business beyond Sydney into Brisbane and Melbourne, with plans for world domination.

A philanthropist and passionate campaigner, Zahrina loves to give back to the community. After winning the Commonwealth Bank Women in Focus essay competition, she travelled to the Northern Territory to volunteer for nine days in a remote aboriginal community with the Moriarty Foundation. Her journey ignited her desire to make a difference to the literacy levels within the Australian Indigenous community. The trip spawned a series of presentations and a children's photographic book entitled *'Zahrina and Tina's Outback Adventure Book'*, in which she shares her experience using both story and images.

In November 2014 Zahrina travelled to New York where she photographed celebrity Aviva Drescher from the Real Housewives of New York City, as well as other dynamic international entrepreneurs.

While Stateside, Zahrina conducted workshops at the Australian Consulate and addressed New York networking communities on personal branding. This trip saw her expand her business internationally to include personal branding shoots in New York as well as her pre-existing photography studios in Sydney, Melbourne and Brisbane.

"Whatever you do, be different – that was the advice my mother gave me, and I can't think of better advice for an entrepreneur. If you're different, you will stand out."
Anita Roddick

Kathy Ashton Bio

International award winning business person and author, Kathy Ashton understands that the health of your business is reflected and influenced by your own health. Kathy teaches which foods benefit the mind and body.

As a nutritional medicine practitioner she believes that the gut is nothing short of a miracle, and when it is healthy, your brain and mindset are also healthy. Kathy's motto: the miracle gut = a miracle 'me' (m = mind, and e = emotions).

Using whole food, plant based, oil free foods she sees her patients produce amazing results, transforming their energy levels, sleep patterns, they lose weight and become pain free.

Through her programs, *My Healing Kitchen* events and clinic work, Kathy believes that change in your health, is a journey from fork to mouth and is only one small decision away.

Nipples to Nowhere – One Woman's Journey of Health and Recovery

Kathy Ashton – Australia

As I sit here getting ready to write this I wonder to myself, where on earth do I begin. My health story, or my health journey, like many other women is complicated, long winded and a little scary at times.

As I write this I do not have nipples, I lost them, how careless of me I hear you say... and my thoughts exactly. In actual fact I have lost both my boobs too... super careless I know.

Back in 2014 I had a double mastectomy due to a diagnosis of Ductal Carcinoma In Situ. I will explain all this further in my story, but for now, all I need to say is I am a Nipple-less woman due to my medical insurance telling me that an operation to put my nipples back was not covered.

You see, I had planned on having a full breast reconstruction, and of course, that includes nipples. Most people are born with nipples, they are an integral part of the breasts. My son tells me however that I don't need nipples any more, given my children are all in there 20's! Not needed anymore Mum they say we have truly finished with them … very funny. This journey has been a long one.

It started when I was just 34 years of age, my three children were very small and I was super fit, a stay at home mum, with a zest of life and fun. Then came the challenges:

Completely out of the blue, I woke one morning and I felt a lump on my right breast. It was so big my husband could see it. We panicked, so I rang my trusted health specialist, who suggested I go see a breast surgeon that afternoon and have it looked at.

To make a long story short the end result from this was a cyst and that I would have to have regular checkups, mammograms and many biopsies during my life to date.

In November of 2013 my lumps moved to another level, it was so sore I was unable to lie on it or sleep on it and yet again it was another cyst. This one was the biggest though by far. But as usual more ultrasounds, mammograms and biopsies.

The thing that makes this lump stand out, was I thought to myself, I am totally over these breasts. They are totally annoying and I was finished with them. I remember telling my sister-in-law at a family function after this last episode, I was sick of these things, and wished they weren't there – Oh dear, one thing is for sure, be careful what you wish for.

Tuesday May 2014, it was 4 am in the morning, I woke with a dragging feeling in my left breast. Oh no, not another one, I thought to myself. But this just did not feel the same, I woke my husband and said hey feel this. He thought his Christmases had arrived, but no, I wanted him to feel this lump. It was really nagly. He said oh no, that doesn't feel good, you'd better go get it looked at in the morning.

I tried to return to sleep however there was this little voice in my head telling me no matter what you do, make sure you get this looked at tomorrow. No waiting, you need it seen to in the morning. As I tried to rest some more, a memory came flooding in from a very long time ago.

When I was 36, my husband and eldest child went to Hong Kong to visit friends and whilst there we went to Hong Kong Disney. It was a wonderful day riding on all the rides and having fun. Towards to end of the day, we met a Chinese fortune teller, and we decided to have our hands read. I will never forget my reading. He said, "In your 54th year you will suffer a major health crisis, but don't worry you will be fine and live a long life to late 80s or early 90s … no worries, you will be fine".

This memory was more than a memory, I could hear this Chinese man in my head really loudly. He was telling me that all would be ok, but I needed to go tomorrow to have things seen to. I was meant to go to work that day, but rang and cancelled. I then rang the breast cancer clinic and told them I had a lump and needed to be seen straight away. They had a cancellation, and said come in straight away. So I hurried to get dressed and went in.

I did not go in thinking it was anything dramatic. I was quite calm, and was convinced it was another cyst of some description. It was in the vicinity of the fibro-adenoma and for all I knew it may have just been this doing something silly.

I told the 1st Dr that I saw that I did not want to have a mammogram I just wanted an ultrasound. The test result was it was another cyst sitting under the fibro-adenoma pushing that up so that is why it felt so bad. I also had quite a few other cysts that needed to be drained as well. So in came the big guns. The specialist to drain the cysts. Oh boy was that an experience. He was livid I didn't have a mammogram. He started telling me how stupid I was and that really I was being irresponsible and many other things. I felt so traumatized by his berating.

It was at that time I heard the little Chinese voice again, you have it checked, so I agreed. I think my words were, ok then, I'll have your bloody mammogram.

So with the cysts drained, it was not as painful. So mammogram done, I then expected the Specialist to call me in and say, ok off you go. All good, next time though have it first. But that was not to be the case, I waited, and waited, and waited. I was the last person there, and it was getting very late. About 4 or 5 by that time. The Dr called me in and said, not good news.

What …….. What was not good news, what did she mean. She then showed me my scan, and the results were that I needed another biopsy as the little ring of calcifications were a prime indicator of cancer.

I was not allowed to drive home, so my husband who was in the city, came and got me. We were both shell shocked and I needed to wait till the Friday to get the results. The next day I went to work, and one of my Dr's asked me how it went. I told her what happened, the whole story and how the Specialist had been so mean. Bless her, she then took control and decided I would not go back to him for the results on Friday. She would get the results and she would tell me.

I felt so much better about that, so Friday morning came and I went to the clinic. My Dr was in her room waiting for me. I went up, closed the door and watched. She looked terrible, her words were, I'm sorry but it's cancer. You have early stage breast cancer.

What the…..

We both had a little cry, and she then said, right, you are now off to see a friend of mine. A breast surgeon to see what she has to say about it all. I've got you an appointment this afternoon and her name is Katrina.

We sat in the waiting room feeling numb. What were we doing here.

It was at that moment, that my Chinese voice came back in my head, it will be OK you just be OK live to 90……

So I trusted. We went in and the first thing Katrina said to us was, gosh you two have had a rough morning……. come sit and let me explain everything to you, cancer is such a big word…… we felt calm straight away.

She draw me picture and explained that this was very caught very early. The cancer was contained within the cells of the breasts and it would mean that if it was not wide spread she would be able to go in and cut it out and all would be good.

DCIS – ductal carcinoma in situ

I needed to have an MRI to see the extent of it and then we would discuss treatment from there. This was arranged for the following week.

So MRI results not so good. The right breast was riddled. I did not have big breasts but every duct was filled with DCIS. She recommended that I have a mastectomy with a reconstruction. She also recommended that I go see her husband who just so happened to be a plastic surgeon. She said I could see him that night and we could discuss doing everything at the same time. I loved the thought of this, a husband and wife team of surgeons, I thought is was like Dr McDreamy and Meredith from Grey's Anatomy, it tickled my fancy.

We went to see her husband and as we talked about reconstruction and the surgery etc., he throw a curly one our way. As I was telling him a little about my history and about how I actually thought there was a problem in the left breast, he said, if I were you I would consider having a double mastectomy. He said there was a 40% chance of this same thing happening in my left breast later on. He gave us till the Wednesday night of that week to work out should they take one or take two.

So after much discussion on Friday 16th May, 2014, just 12 days after my little Chinese man woke to tell me go and get things checked, I had a double mastectomy.

The operation went relatively well and I woke I woke to no boobs, but I woke to part of the right side skin just above the scar had turned black and was dying. I was told this was pretty normal and I was told not to worry, in a couple of weeks, I would go back in and they would do a skin graft and fix it that way. I asked how long I could have to mend it myself from the inside out, and was told that it was very unlikely that this would happen.

All the time I was in hospital I ate as a no oil vegan. No saturated fat. The hospital was not sure what to feed me, but I told them I only wanted boiled rice and steamed vegetables, salad and a little soup and that is what I got.

And when I went back for my first check up, the black piece of skin had turned pinked again and my Dr had to take me off his operating list for the next day. I told him yee of little faith, and he told me, must be the crazy way I eat. I was just thrilled. My recovery was really remarkable, and I was thrilled.

One silly thing I did was took myself off the painkillers long before I should have. That was pretty silly as one week after the operation I felt like I was being stung by 1000 bees all at once. It was incredible so back on the drugs I went, they were great and I coped a lot better weaning myself off them more slowly.

Four weeks after my operation, I had a small fall in the street. I tripped over and because I was so worried about my new boobs breaking, I held those, and took the fall flat on my face. I broke a tooth grazed the entire front of my face. I looked a mess.

The next day my daughter and I were off on a girl's trip to Greece. We had been planning it for two years and were so excited. The funniest thing was the way kids looked at me because of my face at the airport I was a mess to look at. But that didn't bother me, I was happy, I had these funny blow up boobs and was cancer free.

After Greece in 2014 I got my replacement implants and things felt much softer. So I was much happier. Now just one more operation to go, and that was to have the nipples reconstructed.

The last operation was due to happen in July, however this was not the case. I was so excited, but the day before the operation, my health insurance company decided that I was not covered for this particular item number surgery. I was covered the previous Easter to do it, because it was a secondary part of the operation that was fixing a fat pad, but since it was now the primary reason for the operation it was no longer covered ... sorry.

I mentioned to the very nice man on the phone who worked for our insurance company that it was part of breast reconstruction after breast cancer, and we were told it didn't matter. I told him I thought breasts came with nipples and that it should all be part of the same thing. He said, it didn't matter they were not covered. The number as a primary operation was considered cosmetic.

I cried heaps that day, I was so upset. But after speaking with some lovely friends and family I got over that pretty quickly. I am now nippleless. My son bless his socks, has taken this predicament up with the insurance ombudsman and now I can have the surgery done for $88.

But I am not sure if I want to do that anymore. I have had nipples tattooed onto them and maybe for now it is enough, actually I have only cried three times during the whole experience. I don't like to be blind sided. It is the only time I have cried when I have not seen compassion coming my way.

Many people have called me brave, and have told me that I have handled this so incredibly well, but I just think it is what everyone would have done. It was no different to fixing a broken leg. I knew it would be fine, my Chinese Man had told me that. "You will suffer a significant health crisis in your 54th year, but you will be fine and live a long life to late 80's early 90s." remember!

That has been what has kept me going. I am one of the lucky ones no chemo or radiation therapy for me, it was not needed as the cancer had not invaded any of my lymph nodes, it will never return so I feel blessed.

I feel certain that my guardian angels have been looking after me this whole time. I am not too sure what the lesson is in all this. Maybe it is one of trust. Trust in the universe, trust that my Chinese man knew more than me. Trust that I will live a long and happy life till well into my 90's. Trust that food is medicine. Trust in the power of the placebo. Trust in love.

As a footnote to the story I did get the operation for nipples so I am now the "complete" woman again, thanks to my son and his never ending efforts.

To find out more about these inspiring women and how you can contact them, go to www.nikkitaylor.com.au and you will find their contact details. You will also find more inspiring stories from other inspiring ladies from around the world.

www.ingramcontent.com/pod-product-compliance
Lightning Source LLC
Chambersburg PA
CBHW071927290426
44110CB00013B/1501